*For all my Block Island friends with
gratitude and affection.*

Seasons at Sea Meadow

Published by Book Nook Press
Book Nook of Block Island, LLC dba Book Nook Press
Water Street, P.O. Box 598
Block Island, Rhode Island 02807
www.blockisland.com/booknook/

ISBN 0-9658983-5-0

Printed in the United States of America

First Edition

1 3 5 7 9 10 8 6 4 2

Seasons at Sea Meadow
Gardening and other Pleasures on Block Island

Jane Boone Foster

Book Nook Press

Table of Contents

Arrival

My love affair with Block Island began back in 1910 when, at age three, I spent my first summer here. Back then my father, Captain Charles Boone, was stationed at the Brooklyn Navy Yard, and my mother, hoping to take her two children to the country for the summer, discovered an affordable solution through an ad in the *New York Times* for a boarding house on Block Island ($20 a week for all of us, including meals). And so after school closed in June, we set forth for this faraway place, the great unknown, and I am forever grateful to my mother for her deep-rooted optimism and courage.

To get to Block Island in those days, we took one of the big Fall River Line steamers from New York to Providence. Looking at my atlas now, I see that we must have traveled by way of Long Island Sound, then Block Island Sound, and up Narragansett Bay to Providence. The trip was pure excitement for us, including, as it did, a picnic supper on deck, and sleeping in berths with a port hole for peeking out at passing lights on shore. Next morning we boarded the old Mount Hope, a side-wheeler, and survived a three-and-a-half hour trip to Block Island.

We docked at Old Harbor; there was a steamboat pier then where the breakwater and Ballard's are now. We were met by a big open wagon, pulled by two, sturdy horses driven by a smiling-faced farmer with a long, gray beard, "Grandpa Hayes," as we soon learned to call him. Thus began the first of many happy, care-free summers!

The Farm

The Hayes farmhouse accommodated about twenty boarders at a time, and served three wonderful meals a day, always including for supper (to our delight) two-layer cakes up on pedestal plates. There were always big pitchers of frothy, unpasteurized milk and little pitchers of thick, yellow cream. The main meal, "dinnah," was served at noon.

Our room was large and airy, with cots for us two kids, and collapsible, cheesecloth screens in the windows. We had washbowls and pitchers for bathing, a little, flowered, china "potty" under the bed, and kerosene lamps. The Southeast Light flashed green across our walls at night, the breeze sang through the screens, and we felt as safe as birds in a nest.

The house was always neat and spotless, even in rainy weather when we all used the small parlor, which had an upright piano, hand-smocked gingham pillows on the little couch, and a wonderful windup Victrola with a big horn like the old ads. Imagine, if you can, running a bed-and-breakfast today without electricity or plumbing, heating water for all those dishes in a big pot on the coal range, and cleaning with a broom and dustpan!

The farm outbuildings included the big barn where hay was stored, the cows milked, and eggs laid by wandering hens; several chicken coops and storage sheds; an icehouse down in a hollow, where blocks of ice cut from the pond in winter were stored in the sawdust; a lovely, muddy pigpen with a little dwelling for its two residents, and, of course, two privies up near the house, one for men, and the other for "ladies."

And then there were the wonderful animals: horses and cows, a flock of sheep, pigs, chickens, ducks, and huge white geese, the only denizens we were afraid of. There were always other children too, who became old friends after a few summers. We got into all sorts of mischief, but I cannot remember ever hearing a cross word from the Hayes family, who all liked kids. On rainy days when our roughhousing got on people's nerves we were sent down to the big barn, where we could jump off the haylofts, tunnel into the stored hay, and expend our energy. It's a wonder we didn't kill ourselves!

There was another barn at a distance from the house where sheep were slaughtered, off limits for children, but with a handy stone wall nearby for hiding and watching the horrendous proceedings. Forbidden things seem to have a magnetic attraction for all humans, and we were no exception.

The farm was truly a magical place for children. It opened up another world for me, where I learned to love and understand animals, to know the names of birds and wildflowers, to see sunrises and sunsets and the Milky Way on a clear night, how to swim and dive through breakers in the surf, even how to milk a cow. These joys are still with me today, although my surfing and cow-milking days are just pleasant memories.

The Hayes farmhouse still stands, just north of Clay Head. It is the first big house seen when coming from Point Judith. It was originally larger, with several wings and porches, gradually removed over the years by hurricanes and northeast storms. Much of the original farmland is now part of Bluestone, the sanctuary and hiking trails off Corn Neck Road.

Changes

We summered at Hayes Farm until the years of college and summer jobs put an end to those leisurely vacations, and then during World War II the Island was closed to visitors for several years.

It was during the war years that, married and living in Wilton, CT, I got a job working at a perennial nursery, and began to understand some of the mysteries and delights of growing plants, their foibles and needs, and the pleasure of handling and caring for them like pets. Later, I started my own nursery business, with a small greenhouse and four, fertile acres lined out in six-foot-wide raised beds.

These were busy years, but time was always found for a few weeks on Block Island. In 1949 my husband and I bought Breezy Point, opposite Scotch Beach on the Salt Pond. The little, one-hundred-year-old house was open to the winds and weather, but we were enchanted to own part of our beloved Island.

The Point was old farmland with wonderful topsoil, and I soon had a flower bed on the south side of the house and a vegetable garden plowed out back. It was an exciting place to be in the summer. We had a "cafe' seat" on the big harbor, with boats coming and going, the southwest wind barreling in to keep us cool, and the ocean beach just a short walk to the east. We managed there without electricity, plumbing, or telephone, pumping our water manually from the big cistern, none of it a hardship for me after my childhood years here.

A New Life

However, the war had changed the focus of our lives, and in 1952 my husband and I ended our marriage of twenty years. I remarried a year later.

It has been my observation that second marriages are often very happy indeed, perhaps because the passing years have matured us and made us more understanding of others. I was twice blessed, as I acquired four, young stepchildren who had lost their mother to a sudden illness. I sold my little nursery business and entered into a new life of raising children and running a large household, with continuous gardening too.

Our home was a beautiful place. The house was very old. There were six fireplaces, four of them part of the old center chimney, a big, covered terrace off the living room, a little guest house, and, out beyond the big vegetable garden, a huge barn with original chestnut beams. The formal gardens near the house seemed like my own, as I had planned and planted them for the children's mother before her death.

Those years have given us all many happy memories, shared and enjoyed today: gardening, birding, skating and skiing in winter, a succession of pets including two dachshunds always competing for lap space, and, of course, time on Block Island. Our two oldest daughters were married in Wilton with their receptions at home under a big, pink tent off the terrace. There were bowls of home-grown pansies on all the tables, and the gardens a dream of June perfection. The children are all in their fifties now, my best and beloved friends, and I'm happy to report, all devoted gardeners.

Later Years

After my husband retired, we were able each year to spend seven months at our new home on Captiva Island, Florida, and five summer months on Block Island. Now being "senior citizens" we began to find Breezy Point less than the peaceful place it had once been. So, in 1988 we sold it, and moved further down the Neck to a larger house on a knoll, overlooking a lovely slice of distant blue sea and nearby old pasture land where a few cows still graze today. We called it Sea Meadow.

When we acquired it, except for a mowed area around the house, the three acres were overgrown with brambles, honeysuckle, poison ivy, and various other weeds. Not a stone wall was visible, and the land was a tangle of second growth. Island workmen cleared the meadow and stone walls, plowed out a big vegetable garden for me, and fenced it against the deer. Everything else has been done, bit by bit, over the last ten years, including the cool, gray-green garden for me to enjoy from my kitchen window.

Three years later after the loss of my beloved husband, I sold the Florida house and moved permanently to Block Island, the place on earth where I truly belong, where I have always longed to be, where I am content to stay home. I have many old friends here, my two little dogs for company and amusement, and my gardens to care for and enjoy. And, of course, I am fortunate to have a strong, healthy, full-time gardener — me!

And Now

The shelves in bookstores are loaded with gardening books, as are, I am sure, the bookcases of most serious gardeners. So why another? About seven years ago I started writing a weekly newspaper column called "Garden Notes" for the *Block Island Times*, and, over the years since, have had many requests for their inclusion in a book. Of course these notes were geared to the seasons written, and meandered along as thoughts came to me. I'm afraid that this book will have the same hit-or-miss flavor at times, but I hope that my message will be apparent: gardening opens our eyes to the world around us, brings endless hours of fun and joy to our existence, and reveals to us many truths about life in general.

Welcome to Sea Meadow!

January & February

Under the snowdrifts the blossoms are sleeping,
Dreaming their dreams of sunshine and June,
Down in the hush of their quiet they're keeping
Trills from the thrushes' wild summer-sung tune.
                    - Harriet Prescott Spoffard

Weather

It always amazes me how in the middle of winter my thoughts keep turning to my garden. The little pad on my bedside table is filled with notes, jotted down at odd, wakeful hours, under the heading "To Be Done." But *when* is another matter. How much time do I have? The weather is different here, and predicting the arrival of spring is difficult.

Block Island is small, a little, pork-chop shaped piece of land sitting 10 miles out in the ocean, its temperature somewhat subject to that of the surrounding sea. We are cooled in the summer by the wind blowing over its waters, and protected from frost in the fall, usually until Thanksgiving, by ocean temperatures above 50°. Our springs are often cold and late. Swimming before July Fourth is only for the hardy, but I have often found it pleasant in early October, my favorite month here.

As for winters, who knows? They seem to be about fifty-fifty between ferocious and mild. When they are ferocious, we are snowbound and the boats bringing our mail and supplies don't come, but the Island children have a wonderful time coasting and skating on our many ponds. When they are mild, there are lovely long walks on the east beach at low tide, daffodils poking up early, even the birds trying out a few, tentative warbles in preparation for spring.

I love the winters here. Being into my nineties, my traveling days are a past pleasure, and besides, I would not leave my two little dogs, a constant source of comfort and delight. The Island is peaceful, quiet, and so beautiful! The stars are bright overhead, the moon reflected in the ocean on calm nights, the roads empty of traffic, mopeds, and tourists. Old friends have time to visit and to chat in the post office and grocery store, and there are long evenings for reading and listening to music. Solitude, unlike loneliness, is to be enjoyed.

> Announced by all the trumpets of the sky,
> Arrives the snow and driving o'er the fields,
> Seems nowhere to alight.
> - Ralph Waldo Emerson, *The Snowstorm*

Waiting

It is too early to start seeds, and our gardens are often still locked into winter cold, snow, or mud. As nothing seems urgent, I find that I waste a lot of time just puttering around, a little of this and a little of that, and always a good book to tempt me to idleness. The cure for this shiftless behavior is to make lists, a major one of everything you plan to get done before the spring, and daily notes to reduce the major list by two or three items.

In fact, if you plan your day ahead and stick to the plan (always within reason, of course), the evening brings a pleasant sense of personal worth and accomplishment. In your daily schedule, be sure to include time for exercise and rest, as well as play. Hurry and striving for perfection, both producers of stress, are always to be avoided.

Our bodies as well as our minds must be kept active, it is surprising how out of shape we become when outdoor activity slows down. Being elderly speeds up the process, and gardening isn't much fun if every joint creaks and knees refuse to bend! Walking is delightful, especially on the beach with the dogs, who also need exercise, but if the tide is up and the sand is blowing it is unpleasant, and there are many days when we are housebound. I have a new exercise machine, a Power Rider, which works on shoulders, waist, knees, back, et al. It is fun to use and I find that ten or fifteen minutes a day while watching television does wonders for mobility. It can be folded up and slid under the bed or moved to a closet, but I keep it in full view so that I cannot ignore it.

Catalogues

Planning the garden begins with the arrival of our seed catalogues. This past year some of these came in December, when no one has time to even think of such nonsense, but they were sent again in January in case, I suppose, the first had been thrown out with old L.L. Beans and Talbots. Catalogues make exciting reading! The pictures are a dream come true, and the descriptions assure us that we too may realize the ultimate fantasy: a garden that is superb, charming, stunning, elegant, gorgeous, spectacular, lovely, even exotic. If a plant is said to be merely attractive, could there be something wrong with it?

When it comes to vegetables, how can one make a choice? Burpee offers ten varieties of green beans and four of other colors; Park lists twenty-three, mixed-up colors . The lists are endless, but perhaps a few suggestions will help. I have grown Park's slenderette beans for many years, and have never found anything I like better. They are early (53 days), crisp, stringless, delicious, and, if kept picked (when small, please), will bear for the entire season. Several years ago I grew two new (to me) eggplant: Rosa Bianca and Ghostbuster, a white. Who could resist those names? The first was a disappointment, but the latter was wonderful, the plant beautiful with silvery green leaves, and the fruit prolific and delicious. So don't be afraid to take a chance; grow your old favorites, but try something new.

Seed prices vary, and one must know how many there are in a packet to compare. Burpee and Park are about the same. I have used Park for more than forty years and find them to be topnotch in every way, but I like Harris also, especially for their pelleted carrot and lettuce seeds, which eliminate the work of thinning, and Shepherd lists many old-fashioned varieties that take us back to the gardens of our grandmothers. Burpee, always reliable in the seed department, now offers plants, both annuals and perennials, and some vegetables, including tomatoes, peppers, and eggplant. The prices for these seem moderate to me, considering the time and worry involved in raising your own from seed. Both Park and Shepherd list seed collections with illustrated brochures for children's gardens, including flowers and vegetables easy and fast to grow, i.e., radishes, beans, marigolds.

The ads for meadow gardens are a constant temptation, a lovely idea and so easy: just sprinkle the seed and wait! However, if you read the directions on the can, you will find that the soil must be prepared, and kept watered and weeded, as for any new garden. Cornell University did a recent study on meadow gardens, and concluded that, even with preparation and care, very few survived beyond the first season, and here, even if they did, I am sure that our resident deer would gobble them up, so don't waste desire on the unlikely!

Supplies

Growing your plants from seed has many advantages. You can have the varieties you want, ready to set out at the proper time, and of course it's fun, but don't expect a big money saving, at least for the first year.

You will need a bag of sterile soilless mix, which eliminates the damping-off problem at the source. (Regular potting soil packs down too firmly when watered, and doesn't cling well to the little roots when transplanting. Never use garden soil unless you sterilize it in the oven, a messy and very smelly process.)

Any sort of container is possible as long as it is shallow, clean, and has drainage holes. I reuse the little six-packs from purchased plants, but a friend of mine uses milk cartons set horizontally with one side removed, the ends firmly clipped together, and little holes punched for drainage. All previously used containers should be sterilized by cleaning in a solution of one part Clorox to nine parts water, and then rinsed thoroughly. The use of a nice, shallow kitty-litter box will make the whole process of seed starting a bit tidier!

The investment in a light stand will eliminate trying to raise seedlings on a sunny windowsill, the ultimate experience in frustration. It can be a simple, four-foot setup with two fluorescent tubes, or a larger one with several shelves. I have a three-shelf Flora Cart, twenty years old and not as fancy as the newer models, but the hundreds of little plants raised there don't seem to mind. The stand is connected to a simple timer that provides light for sixteen hours daily. Some seeds need bottom heat for germination, obtained by setting the boxes on top of the light covers.

When

Don't be in a hurry to start your seedlings, as you will end up with a lot of leggy, overgrown plants, demanding constant attention and past their best at outside planting time. Check your seed packages for approximate indoor sowing dates, usually six to eight weeks before the last frost in your area. I find this too early for many fast growers, like marigolds and zinnias, and we must wait for the soil to warm up before setting out melons, peppers, and tomatoes, all fast growers from seed. However, tomatoes may be started as early as late March if you are prepared to move them several times into larger containers. Half-gallon milk containers are perfect for this. Cut off the tops, punch several holes in the bottoms, and set the plants deep, as they will root along their stems. When the ground warms up you can cut off the base of the container and slide each plant into its permanent location, nice and deep!

If you have a cold frame, you can start seeds of broccoli, cauliflower, and lettuce a month earlier than in the open ground. Most other crops do best if sown directly into the garden at the proper planting time.

As we look ahead to our gardening season, don't forget two available and very useful helps, to be used later perhaps, but ordered now while we are in a planning mood. I refer to floating row covers and landscape fabric.

The first, also sold under the name Reemay, is a white fabric that transmits air, light, and moisture, and protects from early and late frosts, as well as many insects. It is laid over the area to be protected with lots of "slack," so that the plants can push it up as they grow, hence the term floating. It is a fine protection for little seedlings, and will also prevent borers from invading your melons, cucumbers, and squash, but must be removed when they bloom so that the bees can do their pollinating job.

The second is landscape fabric, a plastic with little pinholes throughout, usually brown in color. It admits and retains moisture, but impedes weed growth. It is easy to cut and shape, and if covered with mulch will last for years. Both of these products come in rolls, three to five feet wide, easy to store.

Houseplants

Now that the days are getting longer and the sun higher and brighter, our houseplants probably need some TLC. I have a lot of them, valued for their beauty and interest, but especially for their contribution to the quality of air indoors. Did you know that our plants renew stale air and filter out damaging fumes emitted by paints, carpeting, facial tissues, aerosols, and even seemingly harmless items like waxed paper, grocery bags, and permanent press fabrics? Constant exposure to these poisons can cause headaches, eye and throat irritation, even worse, but apparently our plants can reduce the concentration of pollutants by as much as 90 percent. Big green-leafed plants are the most efficient, but ivy and philodendron do a fine job as do those that flower. And don't forget that if we talk to our plants, close-up, they absorb the carbon dioxide we breath out, and return oxygen to us!

It is easy to tell if a plant needs repotting; it feels light when lifted, added water runs right out the bottom, and if tapped out of the pot the roots can be seen to spiral around and protrude out of the drainage hole. Loosen up the root ball with your fingers, shake out some of the old soil, and cut back the long, stringy roots. The plant may be repotted into the same pot if the root ball is reduced in size; there should be space for about one inch of new soil around and under it.

For top heavy plants like aloe and jade, clay pots are better than plastic, but they require more frequent watering, a problem solved by lining the pots with plastic bags with, of course, a drainage hole. Miracle Grow, available in your hardware store, is a fine liquid fertilizer. It is easy to mix, seven drops to a quart of water, and may be used often, as it is very dilute. It is amazing how fast plants green up with this treatment. And save all your eggshells! Rinsed out and dried, they can be scrunched up for drainage material in flowerpots, keeping the soil where it belongs and, of course, adding a bit of calcium. I find coffee filters handy for the bottoms of larger pots.

There is a helpful polymer product available now under various names. Mixed into the soil, these little crystals absorb water, then release it as needed to the thirsty plants. They contain no harmful chemicals or fertilizer, and last for years. But don't overdo it, as it increases the volume of the soil. It is a truly frightening sight to see a newly potted and watered plant begin to rise above the pot rim. A rounded teaspoonful to a gallon of soil is about right for houseplants—fine for window boxes too! Gardener's Supply lists this as Hydrosource. They also have a new potting soil called MooMix which they claim will make your plants "Moo with delight." So far mine look fine but, thank goodness, remain silent.

If your amaryllis are through blooming, good care now will yield rewards next winter. After the last flower fades, cut off the flower stalk about four inches above the bulb, and place the pot in a sunny window. Continue to water and fertilize (half strength) once a month as long as the leaves remain green and growing (pale, weak leaves on any plant are calling for more light). When the weather warms up, the pots may be plunged into the ground outdoors in a partly shaded spot to grow until early autumn, when they should be repotted and rested.

Most of us living here have our own well water, which tends to be hard. If you have a water softening system, be aware that it is less than friendly to your houseplants, and to your garden also. Hard water contains calcium and magnesium, which plants like. Water softeners remove these minerals, replacing them with sodium, which interferes with normal cell functions in plants. Eventually, the sodium buildup will be harmful to all but native seashore dwellers. The solution: put a bypass tap somewhere indoors, and for your outside hose connections, also.

We all try to give our plants and gardens what they need, according to their peculiarities, knowing that it would be vain and foolish to try to make them adapt to conditions we would prefer. It seems to me that if everyone handled his fellow men with the same consideration, the world would be a sunnier place.

Pruning

The sun in February follows the same path as in October,...ah, those lovely, bright blue days, ... but our peacefully sleeping gardens haven't caught on to this, so let them rest under their blanket of mulch, as we will surely have frost and storms in the days ahead. I find this entry in my garden notes for a past February 15:

We are having a cold winter here on Block Island, but the boats seem to be running quite regularly, the sand coming back to the east beach, and lots of seals to be seen offshore up on Spring Street. Last Sunday when my outside thermometer read 8 degrees, I drove up the Neck Road to church at 9:30 and was treated to the rare sight of sea smoke, turning the Salt Pond into a sheet of swirling mist, and wreathing the ocean in veils of gossamer white. By noontime all was back to its normal placid blue. We must be patient!

However, the urge to be outdoors on a mild day cannot be ignored, so let's do some pruning, a perfect time for it as our trees and shrubs are dormant, and will not be shocked by drastic treatment. Unlike weeding, which takes no brains and leaves the mind free to wander, pruning demands deep concentration. Should that branch come off? How far back shall I trim this shrub? Lots of questions! A few general observations may be helpful.

Check trees first and remove dead branches, also those that interfere with walkways or mowing, branches that cross and rub against each other, and any that spoil the natural shape of the tree. Branches are pruned by first cutting from the underside up, about an inch above the collar, the ring of bark where the branch joins the main trunk. Then saw down from the upper side to meet the first cut. This procedure prevents the bark from peeling down as the branch is severed, OUCH!

The pruning of shrubs is similar, the object being to open up their centers to light and air. Summer blooming shrubs, like rose of Sharon (*Althaea*), are pruned now, and to maintain its shape, butterfly bush (*Buddleia*) should be cut back drastically, almost to the ground. It is a fast grower! Spring blooming shrubs, like forsythia and lilac, are pruned *after* they bloom, when big old lilacs may have some branches removed at ground level and the others cut back a bit.

Remove all dead canes at the base of hydrangeas, and give the plants a light fertilizing. To prune them back, make your cuts about an inch above an outfacing bud, which will develop into a new branch. This principle applies to all shrub pruning and to roses also. Our object is always to enhance the growing habit and natural beauty of our subject. Please, never take a hedge cutter to a shrub, thereby reducing it to a green blob of ugliness! Use it for hedges only!

There are many helpful books available on pruning. For further advice and detailed diagrams, consult your local library.

It seems to me that our shrubs are the backbone of the garden, always there, with their own rules about blooming dates and growth. Last fall I planted a 4' witch hazel (*Hamamelis*) out by my stone wall, opposite the big bay window full of house plants. To my surprise and delight it came into bloom the last week in January and its lovely, yellow sprays of blossoms have brightened the whole month of February. I already feel a deep affection for it.

" Faith is to believe what we do not see; and the reward of this faith is to see what we believe."
    - St. Augustine

March

Ah, passing few are they who speak,
Wild stormy month! in praise of thee:
Yet though thy winds are loud and bleak,
Thou art a welcome month to me.
For thou, to northern lands again
The glad and glorious sun dost bring,
And thou hast joined the gentle train
And wear'st the gentle name of Spring.
- William Cullen Bryant

Weather Report

The National Weather Bureau Service defines these "loud and bleak" winds as follows: breezes 4 to 31 mph, gales 32 to 63, storms 64 to 72. Anything over 72 mph is a hurricane, and they further state that it is almost impossible for a person to stand in winds over 75 mph. This is probably all true, but I've heard Block Islanders refer to a storm category wind as "a bit breezy last night!"

Here we live with the wind, keeping us cool in the summer, and running up our oil bills in the winter, when we console ourselves with the thought, "Oh wind, if winter comes, can spring be far behind?" For Shelley, who lived in a milder clime, the question answers itself, but for us the reaction is..."Yes, it can be, maybe forever."

This past winter has been mild with no snow until last week, when a nor'easter blew in bringing twenty-two inches of heavy wet snow, and for me plenty of outdoor exercise shoveling paths for the short-legged dogs, and to the bird feeders. Two mild, rainy days following did a fine removal job, and this morning I found a white crocus blooming by my stone wall. Now it is cloudy with a steady wind gusting to 50 mph, all boat trips canceled, so no mail or newspapers, and more snow forecast. Just a normal March day on the Island!

Crop Rotation

St. Patrick's Day is upon us, and, according to legend the peas should be in the ground. But bear in mind that peas will not germinate in soil temperatures below 40 degrees. They will simply rot and have to be replanted later. If we wait for a week or so for nature to cooperate, there is time available for planning our garden layout, so collect white paper, a sharp pencil, a ruler, and your notes and plans of gardens past, and get to work.

No vegetable should be planted in the same location more often than every four years. This applies to all plants in a family, i.e., tomatoes, eggplant, peppers, potatoes (all nightshades), and ditto for cabbage, broccoli, cauliflower, brussels sprouts (*brassicas*), and peas and beans (legumes). We should also consider how these families affect the nutrients in the soil. Leafy vegetables soak up nitrogen, and legumes put it back; fruiting vegetables are heavy users of phosphorous, and root vegetables eat up potassium. And then, of course, we must respect their prejudices. We read that beets do not like pole beans, and that beans are inhibited by any member of the onion family, and also by gladioli, but are very fond of potatoes, and these two protect each other from pests. All members of the cabbage family, broccoli especially, are anathema to tomatoes and beans, and cucumbers hate to have potatoes near them. It's enough to boggle the mind! Your garden notebook will be helpful in eliminating past and present mistakes in the overall picture.

Back in the sixties when I lived in Wilton, CT, my two resident, wire-haired dachshunds were inveterate hunters of squirrels, rabbits, all interlopers. Their favorite targets were woodchucks: large, savage, burrowing animals with big fangs, who can sit up and pivot their heads around like an owl. One dachshund is no match for a woodchuck, but two working as a team, one to focus his attention forward while the other dives in from behind, can handle the problem to the satisfaction of all concerned, except the poor target. I used to bury these victims inside my vegetable garden fence, and grew my tomatoes there for many years. The crop was always outstanding, and insect free!

Now I grow lettuce every year in a bed that gets a little shade from a nearby shad tree, and set plants in between others all through the garden. I grow peas on my garden fence, and spray the ground outside with Hinder to keep the deer from an early meal. Onion sets may be tucked in anywhere for early scallions, and radishes can go everywhere, as they are ready to be pulled and enjoyed in so little time. I am careful to move tomatoes every year to avoid leaf spot, which can defoliate them by midsummer, and to move my broccoli after a major disaster with clubroot.

Garden planning is a time of faith and doubt mixed together, but just now there is always time to make changes, and later too, although planting should never be delayed by indecision. Our gardens are very forgiving!

How Hungry Will We Be?

When planning the garden, the question always pops up, "How many plants will I need?" The following chart should be helpful, but it refers just to eating fresh and the quantities must be increased to include freezing and canning. And of course we all want some extras for our non-gardening friends. The chart does not cover crops that need space and lots of time to mature, like corn and pumpkins.

Crop	Amount for One Person
Broccoli	5 plants
Beans (green)	15 ' row
Beets	20' row
Carrots	20' row
Eggplant	3 plants
Peppers	4 plants
Tomatoes	5 plants
Zucchini	3 plants
Lettuce & Radishes	As many as you have room for

Birds

It is raining this morning, a soft, gentle rain, with a promise from the weatherman of sunshine by early afternoon. There is a softening haze of color over the distant, wooded hillside, and even the nearby shadblow are looking very rosy. Is it possible that we are going to have an early spring? The birds seem to think so. The finches and cardinals are already singing their love songs and, I might add, eating me into bankruptcy. At the moment there are six pairs of cardinals on the feeders outside my bay window, and ten or twelve goldfinches clinging to the sock full of thistle seed, not to mention all the mourning doves and sparrows stuffing themselves on the ground. I am happy to report that my little dog Barkis has caught and killed three rats there, and keeps a close eye out at all times for further sport.

If we hope for a bug-free garden later, our birds must be fed and cared for all winter, especially now. We don't want them to fly off to some place with a better handout! In spring and summer, 90 percent of a chickadee's diet is insects; the Carolina wren, common here, eats only insects in the summer, and almost all birds gobble up bugs for extra energy during the mating season, and even more when feeding their voracious children.

Birdhouses help too. I have four here, on six-foot posts, designed for bluebirds (I'm an optimist), but always taken over in early April by tree swallows, to me the most beautiful, and like all swallows, fabulous flyers as they catch their diet, all insects, on the wing! They become quite tame. One of my birdhouses is on a post in my perennial garden by a stone wall. The little lady swallow sits on her eggs there, and when I am weeding right under her she puts her head out and supervises, while her mate stands guard on a nearby stake. Last spring I had an influx of English sparrows in March, who took over the birdhouses and drove the swallows away. I now have duct tape over the openings, to be removed when the swallows arrive, usually in early April.

Seed Starting When

It appears to me that the garden operation bringing the most exasperation to the most people is sowing seeds indoors too early. All those leggy, pot-bound little plants must be kept watered, fertilized, moved outdoors on nice days, and back inside when the nights are chilly. If we start a bit later, the soil in the garden has a chance to warm up, and the small plants will settle right into their new home. Seed packets give planting dates in weeks before the last frost. When will that be? I always expect that we will have a frost here at the last full moon in May, usually around Memorial Day. Is your garden high and well-drained, as mine is not? Your own experiences will guide you in this occult predicting, but the following chart may be helpful.

Crops (a few)	Start # Weeks before Memorial Day
Tomatoes	10
Eggplant	6-8
Peppers	6-8
Cabbage, cauliflower, broccoli	4-6
Melons, cucumbers.	3-4

These dates are, of course, approximate, as all gardening is, and there is plenty of room for leeway as light, temperature, and hardening off are all factors in the final result.

How

Planting mix should be watered ahead of time, so that it is damp, not sopping wet. A few drops of detergent added to the water makes this easier. For fine seed, like lettuce, it helps to have an old, clean saltshaker handy. Mix the seed with some fine sand or a little dry, unflavored Knox gelatin, and sprinkle lightly (fine seeds need very little cover).

If you have an old, plastic mini-blind, you have a lifetime sup-ply of labels. The slats are easy to cut with scissors, small ones for seedlings and large ones for the garden. They are impervious to weather, and may be used over and over again. All seeds should be carefully labeled when started. I doubt if anyone can tell the dif-ference between broccoli, cabbage, and cauliflower seedlings at planting time; and looking ahead to planting time, if you buy milk or orange juice in half-gallon cartons, start now to make cutworm collars out of them. Remove the top part and the bottom, fold flat and cut across the middle; this produces two four inch collars, which may be packed flat for storage. When placed over the new little plants in the garden and anchored about an inch into the soil, these furnish added protection from sun and wind, make watering easy, and eventually will become soft, and simple to remove when they have completed their usefulness.

When planting seeds, remember that "easy does it," so sow them thinly to avoid root damage later when transplanting. Melons, cucumbers, and squash should be grown in individual containers, as they resent root disturbance at transplanting time. Peat pots, which may be planted intact, solve this problem. Plant two or three seeds in each pot, and if they all come up, just snip off the extras at soil level.

Fill your containers with dampened mix to within a half-inch of the top, firm lightly, and cover your seeds to three times their diameter — just a sprinkle for the fine ones — and set the container in one inch of lukewarm water until the top is moist and sort of glistens. Allow it to drain thoroughly, be sure it is labeled, and enclose it in a plastic bag. No further watering will be needed until germination occurs.

As soon as the seedlings appear, remove the plastic bag and give them light, preferably from florescents. They should have sixteen hours a day, and a timer will free you from this added worry. When a container feels light in weight, it needs water, from the bottom, please. Lights should be about four inches above the containers to start, and raised as the seedlings grow. A cool temperature, sixty to sixty-five degrees, will produce stocky, strong little plants, easy to harden off when the time comes. If you need to thin them before transplanting just cut off the unwanted ones at soil level with small pointed scissors...voila...no disturbance to their neighbors.

There is a new theory popping up in the many garden publications I pore over. It seems that if you run your hand over your little plants, touching and lightly patting them, they will reward you with healthier growth. I have always known that plants like to be breathed over and I guess most living things like to be patted too.

If you have kept a journal, you will find it invaluable for these procedures. If not, start one now. Include dates of seed sowing, and transplanting of each variety, dates when perennials bloom, shrubs too, records of where seeds and plants were purchased and the results, bird arrivals, weather... the list is endless. Any odd facts will add to your future enjoyment of these notes, i.e., the tree swallows are due to emerge from their nurseries the last week in June, when we shall have them putting on their aerial circus for us at dusk.

Be Brave

I have had very good results growing some perennials from seed, and the small cost of this operation surely recommends it. Last year in August I had lovely delphinium spikes from seed started indoors in April, and all my columbine is seedgrown. This is such a wonderful perennial! It takes up little space, is nearly insect free, self-sows, and adds a light, airy touch to the garden. It is especially effective interplanted with iris. The colors always blend, and the flowers hover like flights of butterflies against the sharp leaves of the iris. Delphinium, columbine, and pansy seed need a week or so in your freezer to break dormancy before planting. Columbine seed should be just pressed into the soil surface, not covered, but the shy, little pansies like the dark for their modest appearances.

> I've watched you now a full half-hour,
> Self-poised upon that yellow flower;
> And, little Butterfly! indeed
> I know not if you sleep or feed.
> - William Wordsworth

Three years ago I bought some seed for butterfly weed (*Asclepias tuberosa*), a lovely member of the milkweed family. It grows wild in dry meadows, a brilliant orange shade, beloved by monarch butterflies, hence its name. The variety I bought was called Gay Butterflies, and from a dozen seedlings, I now have three, sturdy plants, two a bright tomato red, and one a soft yellow. This plant is not easy to grow, in fact I had about given it up when, lo and behold this miracle appeared from underground last spring. Like the gas plant (*Dictamnus*), they have a long taproot, and withstand the heat and droughts of summer, the wind and salt of September storms, and deep frosts, of course not usually a problem here on Block Island. But the best thing about this welcome plant is the butterflies, always two or three monarchs flitting about sipping nectar, and the bees seem to like it too. Like milkweed, in autumn the seedpods burst open and release their parachutes to the wind. I hope they find a new home in my meadow.

Odds & Ends

This is a fine time to check your tools for sharpness, and to reread your power-equipment service manuals. I dip my small hand-tool handles into red or orange paint to prevent losing them in the wilds of the vegetable garden. My scissors too, which seem to have a life of their own, and love to wander!

Clean and repair your birdhouses and face them south, cut pea brush and flatten it by piling boards on top, and save all wood ashes for iris, delphiniums, and root vegetables.

For the gardener, March is truly a busy month, and we have April, even more hectic, ahead of us. Our energy level is higher on some days than on others, and we all need time for loafing. Those "To Do" lists with the items crossed off are a gratifying sight, deserving of a reward; "If this morning I do the laundry, go to the dump, brush the dogs, refill and clean the humidifiers, organize my desk,... then after lunch I'll treat myself to an hour or two reading this book I'm hooked on."

Who has seen the wind?
Neither you nor I;
But when the trees bow down their necks,
The wind is passing by.
    - Christina Rossetti

April

Oh to be on Block Island,
Now that April's there.
> (Apologies to Browning)

And how magical it seems after our long, wet winter! The last few days have been something to dream on, daffodils pushing up, forthsythia about to burst into bloom, the sound of robins at dawn, and long, sunny afternoons. The tree swallows have arrived and are casing out my four birdhouses, with their usual crowd of uncles and aunts to help them decide where to settle, and the male goldfinches have changed in three days from their winter olive to bright yellow. The ocean is blue and serene, the beach perfect for walks at low tide, and at dusk the peepers are shaking their little, silver sleighbells from every marsh and pond. And our gardens are demanding more and more of our attention!

Outside Planting

Opinions vary about the perfect time for planting whatever, but our native flora know better than the experts just how the season is progressing, and will advise you accordingly. When daffodils bloom, all early vegetables may be started outdoors, but peas can wait until the shad blooms. Then, when the purple lilacs and crab apples are in full flower, it should be safe to set out tomatoes, peppers, and early corn. And when the lilacs fade, it is time to plant squash, cucumbers, and eggplant.

There is an easy way to know if your garden soil is ready for cultivation. Pick up a good, big handful, squeeze it into a ball, and drop it. If it crumbles into a loose mass, it awaits your pleasure. Early crops, like spinach, lettuce, onions, carrots, and beets, may be planted outside now if the tilth of your garden meets the test. Beet seed, slow to germinate, may be speeded up by first soaking it for nine to twenty-four hours in a warm place.

Recently I read about a great way to grow leaf lettuce. Lay pieces of six-inch wide cedar siding or old boards on a prepared seed bed with one-inch gaps between them, and sow your seed in the spaces. The soil will stay cool and moist, and weed free. Any foraging slugs will shelter under the boards where they can be picked up, *ugh*, or sprinkled with table salt for a fast demise. This method works well for carrots also.

Seed packets are always telling us to thin to certain distances apart, but an easier method is to plant two or three seeds together at these intervals. If they all germinate, the unwanted lovelies may be snipped off at soil level with no disturbance to the roots of the others.

It always surprised me that so many gardeners shy away from growing melons, which should be started in peat pots in early May. Granted, they are a slow crop and take up lots of space, but the same is true of asparagus and winter squash. Last year I never got mine started, but the year before I had sixteen gorgeous Ambrosia cantaloupe on a raised ten-by-five-foot bed. It has become even easier to grow them, thanks to two new aides. IRT (infrared transmitting) plastic film, which warms the soil and prevents weed growth, and floating row covers that let air, light, and rain through but protect from borers, hot sun, and wind. This cover material must be removed at flowering time for pollination to take place, but may be replaced when fruit is set. Rotted manure or compost is a fine soil amendment, and foliar feeding may be done right through the row covers. The ripening fruit should be kept off the ground to prevent rotting in rainy weather. Use a mulch of hay, or used tuna cans with tops and bottoms removed.

If you have an extra bed or space, you can have some fun by collecting all your old, leftover seeds, both flower and vegetable, and sowing them as a cover crop. Just rake in well, water, and wait for surprises. You may get some very useful little plants before you turn it all under. As Emily Dickinson said:

A little Madness in the Spring
Is wholesome even for the King.

All seedlings must be hardened off before planting outside in the garden. Anyone who doesn't own a garden cart is missing a wonderful source of pleasure and help. I use mine, plus two ancient wheelbarrows, as moveable cold frames. Loaded with seedlings, they spend their nights in my cool garage, and can be wheeled out during the day, first to a shady spot, and gradually to full sun, away from fierce winds, and back again inside when the rain pours down. Some old window screens provide further protection. These carts have many other uses: they are light and easy to roll, even with heavy loads, and may be converted into a handy work space with a piece of plywood over the top.

To Till or Not to Till

Nature never tills the soil. Are we really "improving" on nature when we do so? We all know that both sandy and clay soils are made more friable by an initial spread of organic matter like peat or compost tilled in, but after that, according to the experts, a surface application of this material will continue the benefits as it filters down and is digested by earthworms, whereas tillage disrupts structure, and makes the soil light and fluffy, thus leaching nutrients and hastening the decomposition of organic matter. Apparently, leaving mulches and even plant residues undisturbed produces the opposite effect. Agricultural research sources in Ohio report that after a lengthy trial of "no till," test plots had three to ten times as much organic matter and nutrients as tilled plots.

When these theories are combined with four foot wide beds, either raised like mine or flat, according to your drainage situation, beds which are never walked on, with two footpaths between, the optimum in production and ease is realized. The paths may be covered with weed fabric and wood chips or shredded cedar mulch, whatever is available.

When spring arrives, all you need to prepare these beds for planting is a spading fork stuck in and wiggled back and forth, and a rake to smooth out the surface. The beds may be planted in rows or blocks, and are a perfect size for trellises or A-frames. Root crops thrive in them! And they look so neat and nice, important to me as I look down at my big garden all summer from my deck!

My feelings on this subject seem to be shared by an article that ran recently in the *New York Times*. Plowing is out, nature is in! I quote: "The Indians would grown corn by poking a hole in the ground with a stick, putting in a fish for fertilizer, and then throwing in a seed," but of course they had no rototillers. Ruth Stout, the long-gone expert on "no till," must be saying "Hallelujah" on her pink cloud in Heaven.

Mulch

Mulch is the gardener's friend, and to be successful its use demands understanding. It is an insulator, keeping the soil temperature as it is, so hold off applying it in spring and lighten up what's already there to allow the soil to warm up. If your perennials are showing new growth, gently pull the mulch away from the crowns of the plants, but leave it there in case of more cold weather, sure to come.

Light-colored mulches have a cooling effect, and dark materials like black plastic are warming. Once plants are set and growing, a mulch will conserve moisture already in the soil, but shredded cedar tends to absorb often needed rainfall, keeping it from the soil underneath. Wood chips are appropriate only for paths and around trees and shrubs where they may be left in place. They last a long time.

Soil Improvement

Compost and animal manure improve the texture and fertility of the soil. There are many descendants of the original settlers still living here on Block Island, and I am proud to say that several are my good friends. One of them still keeps cows (pets really) and has lovely, rotted manure available to me, if I can persuade someone with a pickup truck to cart it to my garden. He refuses to charge me for it, but since he is a member of our church here I just say, "Okay, Adrian, I'll put an extra ten dollars in the plate next Sunday." The response, "Fine, fine." The native Islanders don't waste words.

Both cow and horse manure are loaded with weed seeds, and should be composted in such a way that heat will kill them. There is no need to buy the fancy activators advertised in catalogues; alfalfa meal, dusted over each layer of compost works efficiently and fast. The easy answer to the problem is kitty litter, like Kitty Green, which is 100 percent alfalfa meal. Dust each layer of compost with it, and add a little moisture.

Lawns

It has been my lifelong practice to spread lime on the lawn and flower beds about every three years, at the rate of 10 lbs to 100 square feet. Lime is now available in a pelleted form, much easier to apply in a breezy climate. We hear a lot about acid rain nowadays, and I am wondering if here on Block Island where our air is salty, away from the pollution of the cities, we avoid this evil. I have a big, new rain barrel outside my back door, connected to a gutter downspout, and use the water for my seedlings hardening off nearby. This water tests absolutely neutral (pH 7), and my little plants, houseplants too, seem happy with it.

The lawns here are more casual than those in the suburbs of cities, and a good thing, too. Mine have lots of dandelions and other weeds, including areas of confederate violets, which I have been trying to dig out for three years, but now I just smile back at their little faces and let them be, as they seem so happy here with me. All these unwanted invaders of our lawns, including crabgrass, can be eliminated by the use of fertilizers containing weed killers, and even worse, insecticides. They are all poisonous! The use of 2-4-D, a weed killer, is linked to malignant lymphoma in dogs. My television told me this morning that a well-known weed killer will get rid of more than 100 insects, including, I'm sure, ladybugs, bees, praying mantises, and probably the butterflies who sip nectar from our flowers. And what of our children who play on our grass, our birds who eat these poisoned insects, and our water supply? How about my little dogs who like to eat grass, and even dig up worms for a treat? Statements by the purveyors of these products as to their safety are about as reliable as those of the tobacco companies, all drugpushers, it seems to me!

There are alternatives to these shortsighted attempts at perfection, and by now we should all know what they are. For our lawns, of course, compost is the perfect top dressing, but who has enough? As for fertilizer, a simple NPK slow release is the best and safest. Nitrogen gives us the green beauty we want, phosphorous encourages deep strong roots, and potassium cuts down on the need for frequent watering by reducing transpiration. But whatever you use, read the label!

And now on to pleasanter subjects!

New Arrivals

Yesterday I finally planted three miniature rosebushes in my perennial border. The poor things, ordered last fall, were shipped to me when there was still a snow cover over their intended location, and have been living in my garage in the original carton, but dunked in a pail of water every few days. However, they are now in their new home, the roots and tops pruned back to manageable size, and I'm happy to say that some new growth is already visible.

Some plants we receive appear to be "done in" by shipping, but they are seldom so, just dormant, and will jump into growth after careful planting. This applies only to trees, shrubs, and perennials, not to annuals, which should be in perfect health and growth when they arrive.

It seems that all shippers have their own ideas about appropriate packing materials. Styrofoam peanuts are the worst, not only because they are nonbiodegradable, but they blow around and, as even my little dogs know, are hard to catch. I have heard them referred to as "ATs," which stands for the charming term *Angel Turds*. Excelsior makes good mulch when composted, and sphagnum or peat moss have many uses. Newspapers are my favorite, as it is such fun to waste time reading about life in other parts of the United States.

When your order arrives, open it up and plant as soon as you can. Soak the roots of shrubs and roses overnight, and of perennials about thirty minutes. If you can't plant at once, sprinkle or mist trees, shrubs, and roses generously with water and wrap loosely in their original package. Keep them cool, in your basement or garage. Your refrigerator, preferably the vegetable drawer, is the ideal spot for seeds, bulbs, and onion sets. Cover them with a damp cloth, not plastic, and keep moist.

Planting

While digging your holes, safeguard the roots of the plants by covering them with wet burlap. The hole needs to be large enough so that the roots aren't crowded, and deep enough so that the plants may be set at the proper depth, usually visible on the plant, where the stem starts to darken. Trim off any damaged roots and stems before planting. Break up the compacted soil at the bottom of the hole, and mix some compost or other humus into it.

Perennials should be set with their crowns a half-inch below the surface, and mulched as soon as the soil warms up. As with other plants, don't be afraid to prune the roots a bit if necessary. Withhold fertilizer from all newly planted stock unless you use the slow-release type.

If you are planting new trees or shrubs this spring, or at any time, remember that most of them push their roots out, not down, so the width of the hole is more important than the depth. The roots of mature trees will extend out to the circumference of the foliage, and this is true of many other plants, including most perennials. The top twelve inches is the important root area for food and oxygen. To determine planting depth, lay a stake across the top of the hole and set the crown of the plant about an inch below it. Untie the burlap and "scrunch" it down in the hole as far as possible where it will rot out in due course. Any sod you have removed may be packed tightly upside down in the hole, around the root ball, and any leftover added to the compost pile. Leave a saucer around the plant, and water frequently and thoroughly. An old adage goes, "A $5 tree will die in a 50¢ hole, but a 50¢ tree will thrive in a $5 hole."

You should be aware of a new hazard: brown, plastic burlap, which looks like the real McCoy but is lethal to plants if left on. It must be completely removed before planting along with any wire, which could restrict growth. I can't imagine why nurseries would set up a boobytrap like this for their trusting customers.

Live-Ins

Most of us have Easter plants continuing to give us a feel of spring, indoors at least, and they may give us permanent pleasure in years to come if given proper care now. Remember that bulbs have been forced into early bloom, which weakens them, but tulips and daffodils will usually give us some bloom the second year if they are planted in the garden now, after blooming, and allowed to "ripen off" there. Your Easter lily is very hardy, and should be planted carefully like other lilies. After it finishes flowering, cut off the faded blooms, but allow the stalk to wither away naturally, and keep the plant growing in a sunny window with light watering. When the weather has settled, early June perhaps, prepare a hole several inches deeper than the pot itself, in a well-drained, sunny location. Put a two-inch layer of pebbles in the bottom of the hole, but no fertilizer, knock your lily out of the pot carefully, and plant it. It does not matter if some of the stalk is buried a bit. It's a good idea to put a stake or label beside it, as it may not reappear until late next spring. These lilies are often slow to break ground.

Don't forget the houseplants that have kept you company all winter. They will appreciate a little fertilizer now, as the days grow brighter, and remember that they get dusty just as your furniture does. If they are too large for a shower in the kitchen sink, wipe off the leaves with a clean, damp sponge or some wet paper towels. Amaryllis should be kept growing indoors until it is warm enough to sink the pots outside in a shady garden spot for more growth through the summer. In the fall they come into the cool cellar for a rest. We all know that there are just too many tasks demanding our attention at this time of year, but remember "easy does it."

On this small, friendly Island, the activities of others are of vital interest to all, especially to one's neighbors. I favor an "early to bed and early to rise" schedule, but if my neighbors lights are on at 6 a.m., I know that they are taking the 8 a.m. boat to the mainland, going "off-Island" as we say here. Now in spring we look for signs of activity at the deserted homes of other friends, who, like the birds, fly south for the winter, and will be ecstatically greeted when they return.

May

The swallow is come!
The swallow is come!
O, fair are the seasons, and light
Are the days that she brings,
With her dusky wings,
And her bosom snowy white.
        —Henry Wadsworth Longfellow

Or, as Christina Rossetti puts it:

It's surely summer, for there's a swallow;
Come one swallow, his mate will follow,
The bird race quicken and wheel and thicken.

This seems to be a wonderful spring for birds; they are every-where. The robins start the dawn serenade, the cardinals chime in, and the full chorus is almost immediate. Being an early riser I hear the whole symphony, lasting twenty minutes, before the musicians buckle down to the serious business of eating and courting. Wouldn't it be delightful if we humans were on the same schedule?

Jenny Wren arrived three days ago. She is my most welcome guest, as until last year I had not had a house wren nesting with me on Block Island, although I always had one where I lived in

Wilton many years ago. Her constant, joyful, bubbly song lifts the heart! The elegant lady rose-breasted grosbeak feeds on my thistle seed sock upside down like a nuthatch. She is wearing a silver bracelet on her leg, put there recently, I'm sure, by Mrs. Lapham, our eminent bird bander. And the swallows! There are always tree swallows in three of my birdhouses, very secretive just now as they are hatching eggs, and this year a pair of barn swallows are determined to nest in my garage, not easily outwitted. I have a male pheasant who is missing one foot, probably shot off by a cross-eyed hunter. He hippity-hops around, even runs in a wobbly fashion, and can also fly, so I trust he will survive.

L'amour

As Tennyson so perceptively wrote, "In the spring a young man's fancy lightly turns to thoughts of love." Why limit it to young men? At the risk of introducing a note of pornography into these dignified pages, I must report that where I live there are birds thinking of nothing else but! They seem to be courting everywhere. How can one hang out the laundry when a tree swallow is sitting on his mate atop the clothes pole? For the past two years I have had a single, celibate mockingbird here, but he has now enticed a lady from more southern climes, and I am sure that soon they will both be dive-bombing my little dog Barkis as they did old Freddy in Florida. One day last week I nearly hit two pheasants on the edge of the Neck Road putting on a spectacular mating ritual. They bestowed a fleeting glance at my car, but were not deterred from more important concerns. We take it for granted that there will always be little birds, but how pleasant it is to know for sure. Now to other matters!

Lilacs

May is lilac here in New England,
May is a thrush singing "Sun Up!" on a tiptop ash tree,
May is white clouds behind a tall tree
Puffed out and marching upon a blue sky.
— Amy Lowell

When our lilacs finally bloom here, it always seems to me that they are telling us to stop worrying about the weather and late frosts, to start putting away those turtlenecks and other accouterments of the past winter. After all, we have to trust someone to guide us, and nature is always our safest mentor.

Lilacs should be pruned *after* they bloom, but who can resist cutting some branches to bring indoors? There is a double bonus here, light pruning and fragrance wafting everywhere. Unfortunately, cut lilacs tend to wilt, but with proper care and handling they can be kept in fine condition for five or six days.

Cut the tallest flowering branches, using a ladder if you don't have a six-foot man around, always so convenient! Cut here and there, shaping the shrub as you go, but leaving lots of terminal branches for next year's bloom. This is best done before a full bloom and in the early morning. Make your cut one-quarter inch above an outfacing leaf node (where a new branch will develop) and remove all foliage except the two leaves just below the flowers. Cut at an angle and use sharp clippers. Indoors, recut the stems and put them at once into a clean container filled with very warm preservative solution (one teaspoon vinegar and one tablespoon sugar to three cups of water). Scraping away an inch of bark at the bottom and splitting the stems one or two inches with a sharp knife seems to help recovery. Leave your lilacs overnight in a cool, dark spot (garage) so that they can soak up the water they need. Keep your arrangements away from hot, sunny locations, and every three days recut the stem ends and replace the solution. This all sounds like a lot of trouble, so if you prefer your flowers in their natural habitat, as I do, just enjoy your lilacs where they themselves are enjoying the lovely May weather.

Leaving Home

Most of us have seedlings coming along and getting too big, reaching for the light, requiring constant watering, needing, just as teenagers do, to get "a life of their own."

When the weather settles a bit more, choose a cloudy, damp day or late afternoon to transplant annuals and vegetables into their permanent quarters. You must keep root disturbance to a minimum and give the plants some protection for a few days until they feel at home. I like to loosen up the soil first with a spading fork, and have a bucket of sifted compost handy to mix into the planting holes, thus providing encouragement for new root growth. Set your little plants into the ground at the proper depth, a tiny bit deeper than they are in the containers, and fill the holes half full of soil, then water to settle it around the roots. Fill in the rest of the hole and firm gently. (If you put water in the hole first, it will drain away and leave an air pocket under the plant.)

After planting, give some protection for a few days from the drying effects of sun and wind. I have a box of old cedar shingles, and stick them into the ground at an angle on the weather side of each transplant, but berry baskets, bottomless plastic jugs, anything handy may be used. For large areas, the floating row covers are perfect. If you use peat pots, be sure the rims are well buried or broken away, as otherwise they will wick moisture away from the roots. Do not fertilize at this time.

Spring rains are sure to bring out slugs. If you are fond of grapefruit, as I am, you have a ready-made slug weapon. Just set the rinds (with a little pulp left) upside down around the garden. The slugs will hide under them and expire, to be scooped up with the grapefruit shell and composted. Or you can make your own lure (if you are not a beer drinker) by dissolving one tablespoon of granulated yeast and two tablespoons of sugar in enough warm water to fill plastic bowls two-thirds full. Set the bowls up to their rims where there is slug damage. Cheaper than beer, too!

Odds & Ends

In this sequestered nook how sweet
To sit upon my garden seat!
Birds and flowers once more to greet,
My last year's friends together
 — William Wordsworth

The grass needs mowing two weeks ahead of time. My gardens are sprouting weeds, seedlings need transplanting, peas, potatoes, onion sets, carrots, and beets should be in the ground, and everything to be done at once. Who has time to sit in a "sequestered nook" or anywhere else to greet the birds and flowers?

I make lists, endlessly, but for those of you who don't, here are a few tips, just to keep you busy. Obviously, all hardy vegetables may be planted outdoors now: beets, carrots, lettuce, broccoli, peas, potatoes, and onions, and even one or two tomato plants with some protection for an early crop, if you are lucky! But hold off eggplant, peppers, and melons till early June, as nights are still cool, and if planted now these tropical denizens will just sit in the ground and shiver! Wait until then also for planting cucumber and squash seed in the open ground.

Asparagus

Our asparagus bonanza is nearly over for the year and the plants are getting ready to "go to bed" until next May. I stop cutting when stalks become thinner than my little finger, letting them grow up into the ferny, green plumes that nourish the underground roots, much as daffodil foliage does. This is the time to give the bed a good weeding, a dose of complete fertilizer, and then mulch heavily with hay, compost, or seaweed (the best!), and cross it off your list. This year I am planning on a new strategy to fool the bugs, really never a problem for me as my friends, the birds, do a good job, and an occasional dusting with BT (*Bacillus Thurengiensis*) gives further control. To repel them even more I plan to plant a few onion sets, herbs, marigolds, et cetera, in every bed tucked in here and there between the vegetables. To further confuse them, instead of a dozen tomato plants together, I shall set six groups of two at various locations, and one or two eggplant (very handsome) in my flower border. I'm sure my garden will look less orderly than usual, but perhaps it will be more fun.

Reading over my list of tasks ahead makes me wonder if I am becoming a workaholic, so I asked one of my friends and was relieved when she said, "Oh no, I don't think you're half as bad as I am." When in doubt, it's always important to consult the right person!

Buyer Beware

We usually have two fine plant sales here on the Island to benefit the library and the school, and are fortunate to also have an Island nursery, Goose and Garden, with a complete line of plants, including annuals, perennials, herbs, and vegetables, plus supplies for growing them. It is always fun to browse through their big greenhouses, and amusing to see the domestic geese waddling around and enjoying themselves. If you purchase plants at these outlets, you are sure to find healthy, well-grown stock, but for you who shop on the mainland a few words of caution may be of help.

Unless you are in need of an immediate display, don't be tempted by plants in big pots, as they are expensive, not easy to transplant, and take longer to establish. Small plants are a better buy for another reason—they will have a longer season of bloom as they grow, and will quickly catch up to those in larger pots.

In general, plants grown at nurseries have had better care than those sold at discount stores or markets. But no matter where you buy them, look for compact plants with good leaf color, not limp or wilted-looking or straggly. A root-bound plant feels light in weight, and has a mass of roots coming out the bottom of the pot. Pass it by. But not too small either! If the leaves of the plant extend to the edge of the container, it is probably just right for planting. And do check the underside of the leaves for insects.

There is always a temptation to buy a few big tomato plants with little, green tomatoes visible, poor things, and it is true that by so doing, you may have two or three for dinner ahead of your neighbors, but the strength of the plant lies therein, and it will never reward you later as a healthy young plant will. As for stunted cauliflower plants with a little, white button showing in the center... well, enough said!

Children

Memorial Day takes us all back along memory lane, mostly to pleasant thoughts. I like to remember my gardens of the past. My first was not really a garden at all, but a clump of old lilacs in my grandmother's yard, a magical place where a three-year-old city child could hide away from the busy, demanding grown-up world, listen to the little birds (probably English sparrows), and peek through a knothole in the fence to see chickens scratching next door. It was my secret place, and I think of it as perhaps the start of the subsequent curiosity and pleasure I still have for the out-of-doors. So let us not forget the children growing up here in this magical place. The knowledge of birds and plants and love of nature can be a gift beyond price from their parents.

To dig and delve in nice clean dirt
Can do a mortal little hurt.
       — John Kendrick Bangs

All children seem to have a natural affinity for DIRT. No one can judge the consistency of soil to make mud pies as they can; they slog through mudpuddles, track up the floors, and are generally not in favor of being scrubbed. They have an advantage over grown-ups as they are down there near the ground, the EARTH, and their endless curiosity misses very little. By the time they are five or six they can have a little garden of their own, and it will always be a bright memory for them, and a reminder of the fun and peace to be found there. It will teach them patience and gentleness, seldom found on television where even in the cartoons it is okay to "bop" people on their heads!

Start them off with a few seeds like radishes, which come up so fast and taste so good, and perhaps a row of green beans, a hill of zucchini, and some onion sets, like little soldiers in a row. Then a few marigold plants will brighten the scene and teach them about watering, et cetera.

Both Park Seed and Shepherd list seed collections with illustrated brochures for children's gardens, including flowers and vegetables fast and easy to grow. The children will soon know what they want.

Children can be very helpful to the older gardener, but don't make it a "must-do chore." A little stipend helps. Years ago I used to pay my kids a nickel for every coffee can of little stones they removed from the flower beds. The competition was fierce, and fun for all ages.

Looking Up —Clematis Vines

Our gardens fill up with such dizzying speed, and we always want more. But where will I put the new plants ordered during the winter, and, as they say, "to be shipped at planting time"? Fortunately, I always have space to heel them in somewhere down in the big garden until I can divide and reset or eliminate some of the present denizens.

One solution for the acquisitive urge is to look up instead of down. Walls, fences, and even trees and shrubs, can be made lovelier by the use of vines, which give us the opportunity to look into the heart of a flower, and can throw a veil of greenery over any bare and unsightly object. There are many vines, hardy for our area, i.e. the old and new varieties of clematis, which should satisfy the most demanding gardener.

To grow clematis is to love it, but it requires patience. It may take two seasons to really settle in and be at home with you. Once established care is minimal.

Clematis may be planted anytime, but spring is really best. Plants are available then at many garden outlets or may be ordered from growers. All mine came from White Flower Farm.

To plant a clematis, dig your hole two feet across and two feet deep, breaking up any hardpan at the bottom with a crowbar, as good drainage is all-important. Fill in the hole with a mixture of good garden soil, compost or some form of humus, even peatmoss, and add a handful of bonemeal.

A neutral pH is best for clematis, so add lime if necessary, in fact a little lime always seems to agree with them. Set your plant deep with the crown three to four inches below the surface, as the dormant buds will take over in case of a catastrophe aboveground, and will make for a fuller plant. Water thoroughly and be patient, as this plant sometimes takes a full season to establish itself. Clematis demands a cool rootrun, so mulch around it with wood chips, flat stones, and even a ground cover, like ajuga.

The vines must have some sort of support, a trellis or wire, as they climb by wrapping their tendrils around the nearest available object. They may be trained to grow along the top of a stone wall if given some wire mesh to cling to. If you are planting a clematis to climb a tree or shrub, set it on the shady side near the drip line so that it will grow toward the light, and give it some help with a leaning stake or string.

Established clematis, which blooms in early summer, may be pruned now, as it blooms on new wood. Cut it back to the second set of buds. Earlier bloomers should be pruned after flowering, and will usually give a second bloom late in summer. Paniculata, the lovely little fragrant white clematis that blooms in the fall, should be cut back drastically now. It will swiftly make a veil of green over everything nearby.

Catalogues sometimes advise spring or fall pruning, depending on the variety, but after more or less doing it when I thought of it, I have come to the conclusion that it doesn't matter. Clematis will take a certain amount of time to bloom after pruning, so for spring bloom prune in the fall, and for late summer, prune in spring. Of course, if you are growing one up a tree, perfectly possible, let 'er go! Could this be a solution for all the dead trees on the Island?

Occasionally, a clematis plant will be affected by "wilt." I have a John Paul II, planted five years ago, fine the first year, then a disaster for two springs, when it bloomed at the base, then completely collapsed. The second time, I called the head honcho at White Flower, and he told me to drench the roots with a solution of an antifungicide (one tablespoon to a gallon of water). After two of these treatments last fall, this spring it grew to the top of the trellis and was smothered in huge flowers. I shall give it another drench this fall, just to be safe!

If you have a sturdy, six-foot fence around the vegetable garden, grow some of the other old standbys up on it, allowing them to be bathed in sunlight and air, out of the reach of slugs and other ground-dwelling pests. Cucumbers and melons climb by attaching their tendrils to the support, while like morning glories and ghostly moon flowers, pole beans climb by twisting their stems. Do you know that our vines here twine in the opposite direction from those of New Zealand? Vines will best be grown at the north end of the garden, so that they do not cut off sunlight from nearby neighbors.

The Garden Picture

"Small is beautiful" the saying goes, and here on Block Island where most of us have plenty of room to garden, "small" is advisable for other reasons too. We must protect our plantings from the deer, the weather is always a challenge, and we all seem to be busy people, and mostly dependent on ourselves for the grooming and maintenance of our gardens. Better a small, well-tended beauty spot than a great, big mess! However, with careful planning and the use of optical illusion, "small" can be made to appear much more spacious. Having been a painter of sorts for many years, I find that the principles used in producing a successful picture apply also to creating an interesting small garden.

Before we start moving our plants around or laying out new garden plots, some planning is advisable, so make a sketch of the area, preferably on graph paper, and take a few minutes on a sunny day to check the amount of sun or shade you will have. Many gardens originally planted in full sun have gradually become shaded by nearby trees and shrubs. This condition may be partially remedied by a saw and a pair of sharp pruning shears wielded with the unholy glee that all men seem to bring to this job!

First, you will find that gently curving edges and several small bays will make the garden appear larger, also more interesting, and the eye should travel to a focal point if possible. If there is to be a path, narrow it slightly as it moves away, and place an accent at the end, i.e., a special shrub, a garden statue, a sundial, et cetera. My perennial garden is a right angle against two stone walls, and where they meet I have a cedar post with a birdhouse on top and morning glories climbing up. I always have two broods of tree swallows a season, who poke their heads out and watch me weeding. Very companionable! In fact, accents throughout the garden add interest; they may be just your key plants like peonies, an occasional dwarf evergreen, or a small shrub.

Remember that cool colors, like blue and lavender, recede; warm colors like yellow, orange, and red tend to come forward; and whites and grays will tie it all together. But an occasional splash of a complimentary color will add excitement (the three primary colors are red, blue, and yellow, and the complimentary of each is the sum of the other two, i.e., the complimentary of yellow is purple, the sum of red and blue).

When planning spaces for your flowers, avoid the "polka-dot" effect. We all want nearly every plant we see, but self-control here is essential. Plants should be set in groups of three, five, or seven of the same variety and color. Tall plants in groups surrounded by short ones will give a spatial effect. Foliage, too, can prevent monotony. The gray-green spears of iris counteract the lacy foliage of other plants. Avoid the tendency to set all tall plants in the back of the border and short ones in front, like steps. Variety here will keep the eye moving around, and don't forget to leave spaces for groups of annuals to be planted in June.

Old Faithfuls

Early May is the ideal time to divide fall-blooming perennials, as the cool, moist weather will encourage new root growth, and the tops of the plants have not yet made sufficient height to present a wilting problem. A safe rule to follow is to divide late-summer and fall-blooming plants now, and let the spring bloomers wait until fall. Oriental poppies, however, may be safely moved only in August, and iris are best divided as soon as they finish blooming.

Chrysanthemums, especially, need attention at this time. To divide, take up the old clump with a spading fork and shake off the soil. You will see the old, woody stalk with new shoots growing out around it. Break off these new shoots close to the center stalk, taking care not to damage the roots. These may be planted singly, about a foot apart, and if pinched back once or twice before July 1 will make fine bushy plants by fall. Chrysanthemums need full sun. Hardy asters should be treated in the same manner.

Some perennials make such a dense mat that they must be cut apart with a sharp knife or a spade. Just be sure that each division has some roots, and replant them far enough apart so that they have room to grow. About a foot apart is right for most plants of average height.

Many perennials, you will find, have long stringy roots which present quite a planting problem. The solution is simple. Just take a sharp knife and cut them off to about four to six inches in length. When the roots are tuberous as on daylilies, you'll just have to dig, but they can be spread out in a wide hole about four to five inches deep.

When replanting, be sure to set the crowns of the new divisions at the same level as before. Too-deep planting encourages disease, especially crown rot, and too-shallow planting, while less serious, is also often fatal as it may cause a plant to wobble around in the wind! A little compost or bonemeal under transplanted perennials is a fine booster, and, of course, always water thoroughly after planting.

Mild weather of the past winter has produced some lovely surprises this spring. Last summer I lost (I thought) a new clematis to the drought, and also my three-year-old gas plant, usually indestructible once established. Losing a valued and mature plant like this is like losing an old and loved dog. One grieves! But lo and behold, the clematis has three new shoots aboveground, and the gas plant is also announcing its presence, like the phoenix rising from the ashes.

With proper care most perennials are long-lived, but it is fun to order a few new ones every so often. This year I again ordered plants from Bluestone, a fine nursery in Ohio. They were shipped on the date I requested, and arrived perfectly packed, growing in individual pots, hardened off, and ready to be set in place (I usually cut the tops back a little to reduce transplanting shock). Bluestone's prices are about one-third less than those in the fancier catalogues with all those big color pictures, and all plants are guaranteed; telephone staff members are courteous, knowledgeable, and helpful. Their listing of plants is amazing. I found Veronica Crater Lake Blue, an old variety I had grown in my little nursery in Wilton over forty years ago. The lovely name describes its beautiful, clear blue color; and I ordered several for "old time's sake." They also carry a wonderful, little, border-edging plant called Golden Star, with silvery green leaves and bright yellow flowers that bloom all summer. It's botanical name is *Chrysogonum Virginianum*. If this is pronounced slowly with emphasis, it becomes a completely satisfactory expletive for a badly missed golf shot, or for any other disastrous occurance.

Container Gardening

I read that in Europe there are professionals who will plant, water, and groom window boxes and other containers so that they always look perfect. Aside from the fact that no such help can be found here, the whole idea of this seems to me to eliminate most of the fun, just as frozen dinners deny us the pleasures of messing around in the kitchen.

Outdoor planting in containers involves several simple rules, and applies to window boxes, tubs, big pots, or anything you choose, even old tires if your taste lies in that direction, although one does hope not! First, improve the soil by adding one-third peat moss, and one-third sand or perlite to eliminate caking. Put an inch of pebbles in the bottom for drainage, and if the container has no holes, drill some. Next, set your plants with the tallest toward the center or rear, giving them space to grow, and last, apply some mulch to eliminate splashing on flowers and foliage, and to slow drying of the soil. Last year, I planted two big tubs on my deck, and put about three inches of those awful plastic peanuts in the bottom, with excellent results as the tubs were easier to move and the plants seemed to have no objections at all.

Wood and clay containers dry out fast, and must be watered frequently, even daily in hot summer weather. I have two plant boxes that fit over the top rail of my deck. They have sturdy plastic liners with drainage holes, are two-feet long, painted white, and easy to clean and care for. They are my substitute for window boxes.

In addition to the ubiquitous geraniums and petunias, our garden sales here offer a marvelous variety of plants suitable for containers. Many of the most-effective plantings are very simple and long blooming. With a careful choice of colors, nasturtiums and petunias can be very bright, and French marigolds and dwarf dahlias together seem to look sunny even on a gray day. For shade, impatiens is wonderful, and trailing ivy, one of your houseplants perhaps, adds a nice, green accent. Tuberous-rooted begonias should not be exposed to wind, but the wax begonias will thrive there, and tolerate sun too, which turns their foliage a beautiful, dark color. The best choices for windy locations are marigolds, dwarf geraniums and dahlias, nasturtiums, and dwarf snapdragons, all sun-loving and having sturdy stems. And do add some lobelia for a blue accent, better than ageratum which gets those black centers in the flower clusters when the weather is damp. Sweet alyssum will hang over the edge of the container, as will cascade petunias and nasturtiums, and if you acquire a few variegated vinca, you can keep them from year to year. In the fall, take them up, prune back the long tops, and the roots, too. Plant them in a sunny protected spot against the house or a wall. They will be ready to go the following spring. I have six that are now old friends.

A window box or a tub near the kitchen is a convenient spot to tuck in a few parsley plants or other herbs among the flowers, and if you have a window box on the north side, away from the prevailing winds, you can summer your houseplants there by filling it with peat moss or other inert material and sinking the pots to their rims.

As we dream of beauty to come, let me remind you to give your seedlings special care now, careful watering and a little weak fertilizer. I must report that I had no germination from my year-old eggplant and pepper seed, and will order fresh seed after this. I found bell pepper at our own Island Hardware store, and there was one packet of eggplant, buried in amongst other stuff, and "unearthed" for me by a nice young man there. There is nothing quite like the failures and errors of others to make one feel cheerful and optimistic, sentiments I wish for you all.

The Flowers That bloom in the Spring, Tra la!

Memorial Day weekend, the official start of summer for the gardener, is upon us with its compliment of mopeds and bicycles on the roads, boats in the harbor, and town crowded with visitors in a holiday mood. There is always work to be done in the garden, but a few days of rest from labor, and enjoyment of the beauty around us will recharge our batteries for the busy days ahead.

Our vegetable gardens have had most of our attention: "Get those peas in the ground, and the onions and the potatoes," but checking my last year's journal I find that most of these crops were started here about June 10 to 15 and soon caught up with those of the "eager beavers." Vegetables provide our vitamins and delicious food for our bodies, but now let's hear it for the flowers, which nourish our souls!

As with the people around us, there are plants we admire and respect, those we like with reservations, some we do not care for but admit to their usefulness, and then there are those we love and couldn't be without. Of course, some plants do not like us, and just sulk when we try to be friendly!

My flower gardens here are limited in size, so I do not have any peonies, oriental poppies, or ornamental grasses, but enjoy seeing them in other gardens and catalogues all the more, and having grown them in past gardens will never forget what it feels like to bury one's nose in the cool silkiness of a big peony flower.

Gladioli have always seemed stiff and funereal to me, but I grow a bed of them for our church and find that the new varieties have subtle and lovely colors and ruffled flowers, and may be looked up to and enjoyed at a distance. The vogue for double flowers seems to be dying out a little, and I am thankful as most of them are an abomination and a travesty on the lovely, old forms: double hollyhocks like bunches of crepe paper, double petunias like little cabbages with the centers invisible, and new double narcissus, which hold so much water that most of the blooming period is spent with the blossoms in the mud.

Plants that do not seem to like us may be won over by patient care and attention to their needs. One of my clematis just sat in the ground for two years, barely alive, or so I thought, but this spring it has decided to stay, and is now loaded with buds. Of course the big purple Jackmani is like a friendly puppy dog, always aiming to please. Put in at the same time as the others, it is now running out of trellis space on the south wall of the house. Aster Frikarti has also been hesitant to settle in here, but with extra attention and some firm talking to seems happier this spring.

And then there are the plants we truly love, always faithful, happy to be with us, and restoring our faith in the world around us. For me, pansies are the flowers I smile at and talk to. They seed themselves in the vegetable garden, among the perennials, even in the mulched paths. They are never invasive and demand so little, although their friendly faces always seem to be saying, "A little more bonemeal, please." The old name for them, Heart's Ease, is truly deserved. I grow a packet of new pansy seed every summer to be sure of having a few new, cheerful faces around.

The beach plum is now in flower, to me the loveliest of all the native spring bloom, so white and crisp, bursting out of steep banks along the road, every plant a landscaper's dream.

Little Things

What is it about little things that is so appealing? I would rather see a pansy or a Johnny Jump-Up appear in my garden than the biggest dahlia in the catalogue, and the tiny goldfinches, kinglets, and nuthatches, chickadees too, give more pleasure than their larger, showier feeder denizens. But then, we must remember that it was the bumblebee and the butterfly who survived, not the dinosaurs.

We are lucky here to have a road crew who are also fond of flowers. On the Neck Road there is a clump of narcissus growing out of a bank, always untouched by the mowers, as are the beach plum and wild daylilies. John Littlefield told me the narcissus has been there for many years.

We gardeners will never have it all our own way. Even when we are most elated by success, there will be failures; otherwise we would get bored and turn to other compulsions, like golf, or water-color painting, which has a certain affinity to gardening, creating beauty, and without bugs or deer to harass us. As one of our friends at Cheers said, "The world is full of winners and losers. Here's hoping you're one of them."

June

Upon the gale she stooped her side,
And bounded o'er the swelling tide,
As she were dancing homes
The merry seamen laugh'd to see
Their gallant ship so lustily
Furrow the green-sea foam.
— Sir Walter Scott

Weather

This week we finally had over an inch of rain, truly a godsend to our parched lawns and gardens. Now the fog has come, gray and quiet, settling into the hollows and at dusk "pressing against the windows like an excluded ghost." Let us hope the coming weekend and following days will be clear and breezy with blue sky and sea for our Race Week visitors, who have not always had kind treatment here from the weather.

We all have too much to do at this time of year, and who can plan on the weather, especially on Block Island. As Mark Twain said back in 1910, "There is a sumptuous variety about the New England weather that compels the stranger's admiration — and regret. The weather is always doing something there, always attending strictly to business, always getting up new designs and trying them on people to see how they will go. But it gets through more business in spring than in any other season. In the spring I have counted one hundred and thirty-six different kinds of weather inside of four-and-twenty hours."

We who garden by the sea are always facing new challenges, and although we have our times of discouragement we are surely never bored. Perhaps occasionally we forget to enjoy and appreciate our lovely surroundings, fresh, clear air to breath, dew in the morning making jewels of our flowers, the sound of the birds, and the ocean breathing quietly outside our bedroom windows or voicing its rage on stormy nights, and, of course, the fog and the mournful foghorns. I love the fog... it wraps around like a blanket of peace, shutting out the busy world, like living on the inside of a pearl.

Happy Veggies

How does that country-music song go? "I always seem to be running, and I'm always running behind." There is so much to do just now, and the lack of rainfall just adds to the list, although perhaps there are fewer weeds. As I write this, rain is predicted for later today, and the sound of it would be sweeter than the music of Mozart.

At the moment the list of things to be done is frightening. My beans are not planted yet, nor beets, zucchini, or cucumbers, and first the beds will need to be freed of a blanket of chickweed and grass. But peas have little, flat pods, tomato plants are starting to bloom, and also the potatoes; onion sets march in orderly green ranks, and the eggplant and peppers are growing nicely inside their milk-carton, cutworm collars. Asparagus is no longer to be harvested, but the fronds must be enclosed with stakes and surrounded with heavy string to keep them in bounds. The garden cart is full of big seedling marigolds, zinnias, and other plants begging to be out on their own, and the garage is full of dirty little containers to be washed and stored for next spring.

There is an easy way to handle all this mayhem: list three areas where you have the illusion of control, three areas where you still believe you are perfect, and three areas where you consider yourself organized, then laugh!

Soil in the vegetable garden should be prepared deeply and enriched with anything that will hold moisture down in the root area. Compost is the best, and, of course, well-rotted manure if you are lucky enough to have some. Dehydrated manure works well too, but must be thoroughly watered in. Give your plants plenty of room. A few well-spaced plants will more than equal the production of crowded ones, and you will find that weeding and harvesting is much easier, and that plenty of air circulation will make for fewer insects and diseases.

The old saying "if a little is good, a lot is better" does not apply to fertilizer, and too much will kill your seedlings. So apply sparingly, at least four inches away from stems, or, even better, sprinkle lightly in the deep furrow under them, and water thoroughly to dissolve it.

Tomatoes

Tomatoes should be kept well-watered, mulched, and dusted for pests. To prune them, look for the little shoot that grows where a leaf spray leaves the main stem, and just nip it out. Tomatoes need plenty of good food, compost, bonemeal, rotted manure, whatever you have. Banana peels are a fine source of potassium, and Epsom salts will add needed magnesium, mixed two tablespoons per gallon of water, two cups per plant when flowering begins. But no matter how we grow tomatoes or what varieties, we all seem to have good salads in August. Nature is very tolerant!

Cucumbers

O for a lodge in a garden of cucumbers
O for an iceberg or two at control:
O for a vale that at midday the dew cumbers:
O for a pleasure trip up to the pole!
     — Rossiter Johnson

These hot, humid days bring another kind of nostalgia: the longing for a cucumber sandwich, crisp and delicious, and cool. Cukes are easy to grow, and your own may be picked when small and tender, as they should be. The seeds germinate fast, and if given optimum growing conditions, which include plenty of space, water, and air, will surprise you with their early bounty. Here are a few tips: work in two or three inches of compost and fertilizer to the whole area before planting as the roots are long and will reach out. Thin the plants to twelve to eighteen inches apart. Crowded cucumbers are subject to stress (just as people are) and need their air space to be happy. If you grow them up on a trellis or netting fastened to posts, they will be nice and straight, also easy to pick. It is advisable to cover them at the start with floating row covers as protection from borers and cucumber beetles, but remove the cover when flowers appear so that the bees can pollinate. Keep them watered, pick them small, *keep* them picked, and enjoy.

Fashion Note

It is pleasant to know that according to catalogues, we hardworking gardeners are examples of sartorial elegance, if a bit dirty at times. The "grubby" look is in! L. L. Bean extols the weathered look, even unto a "beefy" texture, whatever that means. Everything must be "breathable." I am the owner of an old sweater so breathable that each wearing may be its last. I'll miss it when it goes! Today even the models in clothing ads have a rather scruffy look. It reminds me of how, to be in style many years ago, we always rubbed a little dirt into our new brown-and-white saddle shoes and white sneakers.

Weeds

I think it must be rather nice
To live by giving good advice;
To talk of what the garden needs
Instead of pulling up the weeds.
    — Reginald Arkel

But, as Shakespeare says, with his usual accuracy:

Now 'tis Spring, and weeds are shallow-rooted;
Suffer them now and they'll o'er grow the garden.

A University of Minnesota study tells us that in addition to making you feel good, working 45 minutes a day in the garden can reduce the risk of a heart attack by one-third, so it seems that being a gardener has advantages over being a "lily of the field." What more incentive do you need to get out and pull those weeds?

Even if the garden is too cold and wet for much planting, the chickweed is thriving as usual, and little pansy plants are in bloom here and there where they seeded last fall. They are always more than welcome. I am beginning to have second thoughts about chickweed, as it really isn't deep-rooted, and makes a rather soft, pretty ground cover, which can be turned under in the fall. In any case, it seems to be more persistent than I.

Everyone has his (or her) favorite way of attacking the enemy. I love to weed, and have spent many happy hours on my hands and knees with an old knee pad and a fifty-year old hand fork, looking the weeds in the eye, performing acts of kindness for my other plants, listening to the birds,... no hurry, no decisions to make, just perfect peace, and never a backache from this healthful position. The job is made easier if ahead of time you go over the area to be weeded with a spading fork, loosening it all with special attention to big mats of crabgrass. Small weeds, like chickweed, can be destroyed in the paths with a sharp scuffle hoe, and in between plants with a handy little gadget called a Cape Cod weeder, but nothing beats fingertips for close work. One day when I came up from the garden, my dear departed husband, who had been observing my activities from a safe distance, remarked with a twinkle in his eye, "I wish you'd treat *me* like dirt!"

There is a method of mulching paths (invented by me?) that is easy, foolproof, and can be used to smother small weeds already there. I lay down sections of newspaper, six sheets deep, black print only, and throw all my weeds on them, overlapping the paper as I work down the path. The weeds will not root through the paper, they anchor it down, it may be walked on, and, by next spring, the whole thing is reduced to mulch, including the paper.

I have had several inquiries about getting rid of quack grass (white root) in flower beds. This pest grows by underground stolons, and hoeing or tilling propagates it, as every piece of root will grow. The only solution I know of is to dig it out or smother it with black plastic, which takes time. It grows right up through perennials, and they must be taken up, shaken free of soil, and replanted after pulling out all the pieces of white root. Large empty areas may be cleared by leaving the plastic on them through the summer months, to cook the roots, which can be quite deep in the ground. This is a hard answer for a tough question, but there it is. It reminds me of a rather impatient helper I had back at my nursery in Wilton many years ago who used to answer questions about cutworms by saying, "Well, here, we just bite their heads off."

Unsightly as they are, weeds have a useful function. They tell us a lot about our soil. I am fighting my usual spring battle with chickweed, but I read that its presence is an indication of good fertility, true also of buttercups, while deep-rooted weeds like Queen Anne's lace, dandelions, and daisies are a sign of the opposite, and as we all know, goldenrod loves poor soil, and sorrel cries out for lime.

And speaking of weeds, I ran across the following in *Bottom Line*, a publication I read in the hopes that it will make me smarter in general.

Plant a Tossed Salad

> To cut down on garden weeding, mix radishes, lettuce, and carrot seeds together in equal measure. Sprinkle to the ground from four feet up. Result: the radish and then the lettuce will shade out weeds,... and later the carrots will have room to grow.

If you like to garden without gloves, as I do, the scrubbing up process can be onerous. A green thumb may be acceptable, but not ten grubby fingernails. However, your troubles are over! There is a fine, powdered hand soap called Boraxo, which leaves hands soft and clean, and gets nails, too, with help from a nail brush. This is not a new product; I used it back in the fifties, when we made hundreds of Christmas wreaths at my little nursery, usually barehanded. It is available at our Island Hardware here, an oasis of everything under the sun and a fascinating place to browse. If you want something and can't find it, pleasant help is always there, and if they don't stock it, the efficient owner will order it for you. Thank you, Petie.

Pleasant Short Jobs

Keep an eye on all growing and blooming denizens of the flower gardens, which will benefit from deadheading and pinching, practices not as drastic as they sound. Deadheading involves the removal of spent blossoms before they can produce seed, the ultimate goal of all our plants and the signal to them that the job for survival is done. They will keep right on trying, however, and will produce flowers until frost. Pinching may be practiced for both annuals and perennials. If you nip out the tip of the stalk, side shoots will develop, making for a bushier plant with more but sometimes smaller, flowers. If you remove side shoots, the strength of the plant is funneled into the main stalk, producing the opposite effect. This practice will grow specimen blooms, especially on peonies and upright chrysanthemums. Plants like cushion mums may be grown from a single division by pinching the tips from every three inches of side growth until about July 1, when they should be left to develop their blossoms. But as a friend of mine once said, "Oh dear, July is just when I feel like pinching."

For a change of pace, and posture too, use odd moments to prune off the spent lilac blooms, cutting them in the V at the base of the flower, important to insure good bloom next year. More drastic pruning and shaping may be done now for both lilacs and forsythia, removing about a third of the old wood from the bottom. No crew cuts, please!

Bugs

Loud is the summer's busy song,
The smallest breeze can find a tongue,
While insects of each tiny size
Grow teasing with their melodies.
— Clare

The middle of June always seems, to me, to be the time when our gardens are at their best, lawns green and needing frequent mowing, flowers blooming, and the vegetable garden rewarding us with signs of lovely edibles to come. Unfortunately, like the serpent in the Garden of Eden, the bugs are waiting in the wings and getting ready for their stage appearance. Our weapons against them are threefold: keep them away, kill them in the act, or handpick and destroy them. The first requires barriers like cutworm collars or light row covers (Reemay fabric); the second calls for dusts or sprays, preferably organic. Diatomaceous Earth (DE) is effective against soft-bodied caterpillars, BT for chewing insects, and rotenone is safe and usually helpful. All three products are available from Gardens Alive. I like to dust in early morning when the plants are dewy and the air is calm. I have a Dustin Mizer, and can go through my big garden with it in just a few minutes. It gets the underside of the foliage too. For handpicking you must arm yourself with a jar or can of kerosene to dispose of the offenders.

Here is a partial list of our enemies, and their adversaries:

Cutworms	Enclose newly set plants with collars at least an inch above and below the soil level. These gray worms come out at night, and may be found, usually too late, peacefully sleeping in the soil under the attacked plant.
Cabbage Worms	Light green, velvety caterpillars that chew ragged holes in leaves, and leave soft green droppings where they are feeding. *Ugh!* Apply DE dust or spray at first sign of their presence.
Flea Beetles	Tiny, little, dark beetles that jump around when disturbed, chew

holes in leaves, and whose grubs further weaken plants at the root level. Row covers provide good protection, or dust with DE or rotenone. A good fall cleanup will reduce their numbers the following spring.

Mexican Bean Beetle
A very unpopular relative of the lady bug, small one-third, yellow, with sixteen black dots on its back, chews leaves and eats all but the veins. Handpick or dust with DE or rotenone.

Colorado Potato Beetle
This one has black stripes instead of dots, and lays orange -yellow eggs on the underside of leaves of potatoes and their relatives, peppers and eggplant. The larvae cluster in groups, easy to find and crush. This pest is resistant to most chemicals; try BT or handpick.

Vine Borers
This pest attacks cucumbers and squash, especially zucchini. Butternut squash seems to be immune. When vines droop and wilt, look for sawdust-like droppings and holes in stems, easy to avoid if you cover the seedlings or seeded area with Reemay fabric. Also, you can split the stem, dig out the borer, and bury the stem in the ground, where it will usually heal and root.

Tomato Hornworm	A horrendous critter, three to five inches long, which will attack other nightshades too. The adult is the hawk moth, seen at dusk hovering near flowers, like a hummingbird. These large caterpillars can defoliate half a tomato plant overnight. Look for eaten leaves, but the enemy is not easy to spot as it is the same color as the foliage, and usually hangs on the underside of the branch. Pick off and drop into kerosene or snip in half with scissors.
Corn Earworm	These are the same family as the cutworm; they lay their eggs on the corn silk or leaves, and tunnel into the ear. To control, apply twenty drops of mineral oil to the silks near the tip of the ear three to seven days after the silks appear.

Note: You would be wise to sprinkle some Milorganite around anything not fenced, as this year's crop of fawns are looking more and more like deer, getting bolder by the day, also smarter, as they seem to know when my little dog Barkis is not outside. I find their hoofprints in the driveway in the morning.

Watering

Drip, drip the rain comes falling,
Rain in the woods, rain on the sea;
Even the little waves, beaten, come crawling
As if to find shelter here with me.
— James Herbert Morse

Seasons at Sea Meadow

We are lucky this spring, as the rain has been plentiful, but these warm, windy days can dry out the soil fast just when our plants need it most. The secret of growing plants that can withstand drought is to make them root deep, so when you water, do a real job of it. New plants have to develop new feeding roots, and they need deep moisture to do this. So let the sprinkler or hose run in one place until the water is down at least six inches, and if necessary dig a hole with a trowel to make sure that it is.

I have two soil soakers, a twenty-five-footer and a fifty-footer, which can be laid back and forth in the garden, and will soak the area in about an hour with the tap barely turned on (I hate to hear that pump running!).

Evening is the worst time to water your garden, as the plants go into the night with wet foliage, inviting mildew and disease. I have never had any damage to plants from watering in the broiling sun, although evaporation may demand a little more water. Early morning is the best, so let those breakfast dishes sit in the sink and man the hose!

Once the moisture is down at the roots of your plants, it may be kept there by a mulch, which acts as a blanket and prevents evaporation. Use grass clippings, straw, compost (the best), or anything else you have handy. Peat moss acts like a sponge, and will absorb any rainfall or further watering before the moisture reaches the plant roots, so use it sparingly. Perhaps the best, and certainly the cheapest, is a good dust mulch, which costs nothing except a little muscle and the price of a scuffle hoe. Just work around your plants with the hoe, keeping the blade shallow and cutting off any small weeds that have sprouted. Of course this mulch must be relaid after a hard rainfall, but it aerates the soil and prevents a hard crust from forming, so every drop of rain goes down instead of running off the surface.

No garden seems complete to me without an old watering can or two or three sitting around in strategic spots. They will put lovely, warm water just where you need it, and with long years of use, develop a beauty of their own. As Peter Rabbit said, "It would have been a beautiful thing to hide in, if it had not had so much water in it."

While on the subject of water, if you do not have a birdbath, you are missing the greatest free entertainment available. Anything will suffice if shallow and wide, and it should be near a tree or bush so that the area can be cased for cats and other enemies before taking the plunge.

Our friends the catbirds are everywhere, making sure that we know winter is over at last. They supervise my every move in the garden, and frolic in the birdbath at twilight, as do the robins too, whose speckled breasts remind us that they are of the thrush persuasion.

Iris Woes

All over the Island the pink and white rugosa roses have come into bloom, almost overnight, and our flower gardens are full of blooming perennials. Iris should be at its best, but this year such is not the case. I have had several questions about clumps of healthy, green leaves with few or no blooming stalks, and in my own garden, too, this is occurring. My iris was all divided and replanted two years ago. Who knows the cause of this? I think that perhaps a bitter, cold winter may be the culprit, blasting the flower buds which are close to the surface of the soil. Oriental poppies, deep-rooted, are gorgeous this year, and columbine, veronica, and clematis on my stone wall are putting on a spectacular show. All Asiatic and oriental lilies have developed into huge clumps, loaded with buds. This largesse must be a result of the deep snow cover and steady frost of the winter months, conditions just not to the taste of our iris.

> All green and fair the Summer lies,
> Just budded from the bud of Spring,
> With tender blue of wistful skies,
> And winds which softly sing.
> — Susan Coolidge

June is a lovely month, but somehow not my favorite, as there is just too much to do. When will there be a lull? Certainly not yet with some vegetables not planted, some areas not weeded, the grass growing too fast, a few plants still in their little six-packs, not yet set out, even some seedlings growing under the florescents. But looking back in my journal I see that this has happened in previous Junes. And somehow by July Fourth, peace had returned. Well, hope springs eternal!

Nonedible Delights

Let us now turn briefly to a pleasanter subject: flowers. You can prolong the blooming season of garden phlox if you pinch out the tips of some shoots, preferably at the front of the clump, as they will be shorter when they bloom. Plant gladiolas now and twice more at two-week intervals for extended bloom. Sow a few flower seeds in between tulips for later bloom: nasturtiums, dwarf marigolds, phlox drummondi, calendulas, to name a few fast growers. This is the time of poppies, iris, veronicas, and perhaps my favorite, columbines. They do well for me, self-sow, and always look happy, hovering above their lovely foliage like little birds about to fly off. Many years ago when I lived in Wilton, there was a big rock ledge in our lower field, and always, early in spring, a clump of wild columbine, dainty and shy with yellow petals

Jane tending to container-grown tomatoes and flower pots on the back porch of Sea Meadow.

The garden at Sea Meadow.

Sun-lit spider webs spun along the porch at Sea Meadow.

Iris, snapdragon, petunia and many other garden favorites are framed by a picturesque Block Island stone wall.

Lilies of vibrant color blooming in Jane's garden.

Jane with companions Barkis and Olivia during a breezy
walk on a Block Island beach.

shading to orange-red at the spurs. I like to think that it is still there, tucked into a hollow against the warm rock, if its home hasn't gone the way of the bulldozer.

Roses

> It is the month of June,
> The month of leaves and roses,
> When pleasant sights salute the eyes
> And pleasant scents the noses.
>   — N.P. Willis

Mr. Willis appears to be a minor poet of the nineteenth century, but major or minor he commands our instant respect for his inspired rhyming of roses and noses.

Indeed, June is the month of roses. Enjoy their glorious blooms and lush, green leaves, but remember that the hot, humid days of summer lie ahead. Our roses must be kept healthy so that they can build up vigor for years of future blooming. Black spot and mildew are the enemies waiting to attack. Remove faded flowers and spotted or yellowing leaves, and put them in the trash, not the compost. You can control both black spot and powdery mildew by a baking-soda spray, put on the earlier the better. The recipe is simple: a tablespoon of baking soda to a gallon of water, plus a few flakes of Ivory soap (just enough to make the water gray) to make the spray stick to the leaves. A brisk spray with plain water in the early morning, after a hot, humid night will wash off black spot spores and any lurking spider mites. Then use the baking soda spray on the wet leaves. This treatment also works well on phlox and lilacs, both subject to powdery mildew.

Climbing roses and ramblers should be pruned when they stop heavy blooming. The general procedure is to remove all dead, weak, or superfluous canes, and to cut back the remaining ones. Heavy pruning will result in larger and fewer flowers, and vice versa. If you are growing hybrid varieties, any suckers that develop below the joint of the rootstock should be "wrenched" off. Hybrid teas should be pruned in spring, removing any winter-damaged tips. When pruning, be sure your tools are sharp. Make the cut about one-quarter inch above an outfacing bud or leaf joint, and slant the cut down away from the bud, for drainage.

Flowers for Late-Summer Bloom

By now the vegetable garden should be thoroughly under control, if ever, the cleanup work on the flower borders done, and as we complacently munch on asparagus and garden lettuce while waiting for the crabgrass and Japanese beetles to arrive, let's make a last minute check on the annuals situation. The rush of garden work in May, and the glory of spring bloom in the perennial border too often make us forget the long, hot months to come, when we shall want to take it easy and fill the cool house with flowers. But there is still time to dip the tardy brush into nature's paint box, and splash some color into the late summer garden. Quick-growing annuals are the answer, and though planted late and requiring a little more care, they repay us by rushing into bloom as quickly as they can, in an effort to set seed before frost signs their death warrant.

Seeds of these annuals may be planted where they are to bloom, in groups in the border and in rows in the cutting garden, even in between vegetables. The area to be planted should be raked smooth, and thoroughly watered at least two hours ahead. Sow the seed thinly a little deeper than in spring and cover with sifted soil. Fine seed is easier to sow if mixed half-and-half with sand. To prevent a hard crust from forming on the surface, mulch with a thin covering of sand or sifted peat, which can be kept watered with the fine spray from the hose without washing out the newly planted seeds.

And watering is necessary, both during the period of germination and afterwards, until the new little plants have put their roots down far enough to stand on their own feet. But once they have germinated, don't just sprinkle, as this will bring the roots to the surface in search of a drink, and the hot, dry days of July and August will make an early end of your fall color picture.

For the front of the border, especially, there are many annuals that may be planted in June. Perhaps this is because, being low-growing, they do not have to waste so much time growing stalks, but can get right to work on the flower department. Dwarf zinnias and sweet alyssum will bloom in about five to six weeks from seed. Candytuft and phlox drummondi are both lovely to see and quick to bloom, perfect for those empty spaces where the tulips are no more. Portulaca will blossom in about three weeks from time of sowing, and thrives in hot, dry locations. Try some of this in the rock garden, especially the double pastel variety. African and French marigolds take a little longer, about eight weeks, but are well worth the effort as they will bloom profusely until frost, and being natives of Mexico they can take the heat. Nicotiana is perhaps the best quick grower for shady spots. If you once plant this fragrant annual, you will never be without it, as it self-sows all over the place. And don't forget the calendulas, which thrive on heat and drought and are at their most beautiful best in September.

Other Friends

Our perennials are so reliable and tolerant of neglect that we tend to forget that they too need our loving care. The iris look very bedraggled and sad. Cut back the faded flower stalks, but do not divide or disturb the plants until the end of the month. I used to cut off the seedpods of all perennials, annuals too, but have found that a little messiness yields great rewards, like finding columbine plants here and there, lots of snapdragon seedlings peeking out from under the daylilies at the back of the border, and always alyssum everywhere to dig up and move around. Pansies come up in the paths, and who could be heartless enough to treat them like weeds? "From their recent hiding places, smile the little pansy faces."

It is a wise move to label bleeding hearts and poppies, as they will soon go dormant and disappear. Annuals may be sown close to them, but nothing permanent. The ants on your peonies are harmless, they are just collecting the sweet nectar from the flowers.

If you have a shady, moist spot for them, houseplants will benefit from a summer vacation outdoors. They can be repotted now, and the pots sunk up to the rims. If you put an inch or two of pebbles under them, they won't root down into the ground. If you have any old clay pots, do use them. They let air and moisture enter the soil for happy plants.

I have just returned from a reunion at my old alma mater over on the Hudson, a beautiful campus with century-old trees, sweeping green lawns and lovely, colorful plantings. There is a magical place tucked away behind the science building, not easily discovered, but a loved and familiar oasis to all old grads. I refer to the Shakespeare Garden, on a slope down to a low wall and a running brook, the whole enclosed by tall hedges, with raised beds on each level, containing only plants mentioned by Shakespeare. The list is long, and the garden was ablaze with color: foxglove, sweet william (*Dianthus barbatus*), peonies, roses, blue flax, iris, pansies, violas, and many herbs. The garden is a haven of peace, where the birds sing, the little brook murmurs, people speak in low voices, and the world of today seems far away. It lifted my heart to know that such a loved place of so many years ago is still there, as beautiful and unchanged as ever.

July

Be not afraid; the isle is full of noises,
Sounds and sweet airs that give delight and hurt not.
Sometimes a thousand twanging instruments
Will hum about mine ears; and sometimes voices,
That, if then had waked after a long sleep,
Will make me sleep again: and then, in dreaming,
The clouds methought would open, and show riches
Ready to drop upon me; that, when I waked,
I cried to dream again.
- William Shakespeare, *The Tempest*

What a perfect description of our Island in summer; the lovely bird calls, the cacophony of music in town, the sleepy summer days, and the gardener's longing for rain! In spite of the drought, really serious at the moment, most gardens seem to be surviving in a state of suspended animation. We who have our own wells are lucky, as we can use a little water where we must, but gently, gently as all water may lower the water table. I use soil soakers on the vegetable beds, and hand-water tomatoes, peppers, et cetera. with a bucket and a coffee can. The water goes where needed and is not wasted on paths or by evaporation from sprinklers. Last year at this same time we had a spell of very humid weather with temperatures well up in the nineties, but everything survived, including us.

Just now the birds are at their busiest and noisiest, so much to do with all those hungry children, and so many songs to be sung. They wake me at 4:45 a.m., sound the alarm clock for about twenty minutes, and then get down to the business of the day. Baby birds are everywhere. As I write this, there are two young robins in the birdbath, having a lovely frolic, one with a little silver bracelet on his leg, and the male, resident mockingbird sitting on a tree branch, looking for mischief. He imitates my little dog's bark to perfection, driving him nearly beserk!

Don't forget that goldfinches breed and raise their young in July, and still need thistle seed if you have it. It seems to me that the birds teach us the true meaning of independence, not the possession of many things, but the wanting of so few.

There is much to see along our roadsides these days, as we drive to town at a slow crawl to avoid the joggers, mopeds, and the family bikers who line up with Daddy in the lead, the children next, and Mommy bringing up the rear, just like the Canada geese who must be the most devoted parents in the world.

Wildflowers

Our Block Island wildflowers make their appearances right on schedule, as always, and many of them are the forebears of the flowers we have in our gardens, featured in our catalogues and bought and paid for by us. The black-eyed Susans are rudbeckias, the origin for the coneflowers we grow, and our wild asters, whose lovely lavender-blues and white, starry flowers brighten our autumn roadsides, are the origin of the Michaelmas daises, so beloved by English gardeners. Last fall, down a little lane on the Neck, I found a stand of these asters, unusually deep in color, and dug out a clump for my perennial bed. It made itself at home quickly, and is growing happily now, apparently not bothered by the drought. Perhaps I have something as good as Aster Frikarti, a finicky grower for me.

One wildflower that seems to be taken for granted by us is perhaps the loveliest of all, our water lilies, which float on our many ponds like the lotuses in the Gardens of Shalimar. Luckily they are not easily collected by tourists, who seem hesitant about wading into black water and sinking up to their knees in mud.

Some of the goldenrod are already showing color, particularly the little ground creepers, as pretty as anything in our rock gardens. We have many varieties of goldenrod here. The tall ones are at their best when they mingle with the fragile flowers of blue chicory on cool, gray mornings. Incidentally, goldenrod does not deserve its evil reputation as a cause of allergies, just because it blooms and grows with ragweed, the true culprit.

Many of our native trees and shrubs, especially the shad, are now producing berries, and birds are everywhere. In church last Sunday we heard a lovely solo about God's eye being "on the sparrow." I regret to report that Sunday afternoon one of these escaped His notice, but not my little dog's, who had a new toy that squeaked and moved. There was no way that I could rescue it, but I was relieved that it wasn't a baby catbird or cardinal. Am I a bird racist?

Lazy Hazy Days

We take cold showers and ocean dips to keep cool in this hot season, and our pets and birds are entitled to the same comfort. My two little dogs, Barkis and Olivia, get dunked in a bucket of cool water several times a day, and the birds are always in the big birdbath outside my bay window, sipping and splashing, even wagging their tails like the dogs. Happiness reigns!

Fortunately for us, most of our flowers and vegetables seem to have a built-in defense against drought. They put themselves into a catatonic state of inaction, and wait, another instance of nature's resilence and patience. So if you can't water deeply and often, let them be. Don't spray for pests, and especially don't fertilize.

One exception for this treatment in the flower garden is the judicious use of pruning and pinching, which cuts down on evaporation and insures continuing bloom later in the season. It should be done now. Sprawling petunias may be cut back by one-third. All seedpods should be removed, unless you want little seedlings here and there, which you will have anyway, as our plants have minds of their own on this subject. I use grass shears to cut back alyssum, perennial candytuft, nepeta, and any other low-growing plant with lots of spent blooms. Phlox, especially, should have its seedpods removed, as they tend to drop to the center of the clump, where they germinate and revert to that old "pinky-purple," choking out the fine hybrids that spawned them.

On bravely through the sunshine and the showers!
Time has his work to do, and we have ours.
    — Ralph Waldo Emerson

And the more he does, the more we have piled on us! But by now our tasks should be slacking off, giving us welcome rest from our labors. As Jane Austen observed, "To sit in the shade on a fine day and look upon verdure is the most perfect refreshment."

July Fourth weekend is a time to stop work and have fun, and what better place for fun than Block Island, where all the activities are almost within walking distance.

Perhaps our gardens, too, will enjoy a respite from our endless ministrations, so for a day or two let the weeds grow and the bugs chomp away, especially as there are other guardians on constant watch for them. My gardens are full of baby catbirds, robins, and hovering tree swallows, and I suspect that, undisturbed by humans, they eat up a lot of pests, and unfortunately a few nice worms too.

And weeding demands such serious choices! Shall I pull out that little snapdragon that has seeded too close to the iris clump, and what about these mats of white alyssum? We must be fairly ruthless, remembering that little plants will get bigger. Most of us plant our seedlings too close together at the start. A single zinnia needs at least a square foot of space to be at its best in August. But I always have petunia seedlings in little bunches and never touch them, as they seem to enjoy close company, and although the flowers are small the color range is lovely, shading from white to pink, lavender, and fuschia. They seem to enjoy the heat and drought of summer, and like pansies are undemanding and welcome guests anywhere, even in the vegetable garden.

Vegetable Woes and Wonders

The great zucchini menace is looming up. I sometimes wonder why I grow this vegetable at all, but have learned to plant just two or three hills and pick it small. A six-inch zucchini can grow into a baseball bat overnight, or so it seems, and everyone offers it, like unwanted kittens.

Many of the vegetables we grow are now offered in the markets, and they reinforce all the reasons for growing our own. The store beans are past their small tender best, the parsley is limp, the eggplant is not rockhard, the carrots have no feathery tops, the beets, if available, have no tops at all, and I prefer not even to discuss wax-coated cucumbers. The potatoes are very good; I am happy to buy them until my own mature. But one of the greatest advantages of growing one's own vegetables is the fun of trying new varieties, not available in the markets. This year I have three new varieties of eggplant, raised from seed.

Eggplant and peppers do not need a lot of fertilizer, but both will benefit from magnesium, a plant food they need to set fruit. This is easy to provide. Mix two tablespoons of Epsom salts to a gallon of water, shake well, and pour into a handy spray bottle. Spray the plants when they first bloom and again ten days later. You will see almost immediate improvement in the color of the foliage.

My peas are now a past pleasure, and I'm *afraid* to say may remain so. I say *afraid* as I am sure my feelings about them will be heresy to most of my readers, but it seems to me that they take up a lot of space for the output, have to be shelled (harder on the fingernails than "pinching"), and I happen to like frozen peas, always available at the market. The lettuce I planted in between my broccoli and pepper plants is still crisp and delicious, enjoying the cool, partial shade from its taller neighbors. If you have a shady corner somewhere, sprinkle a few foxglove and sweet william seeds around for nice little plants to set out in September. They will bloom next spring.

Looking Ahead

Late July and August are times of bounty from the garden, largesse that pays us back for all the work and seedling care of spring. It is hot, we have a succession of guests, and if we choose to avoid the sun and crowds at the beach, a shady nook and a good book beckon us. But I always seem to find that the vegetables we harvest in late September and October are the tastiest and the most enjoyed. So take an hour or two in the early morning or late in the afternoon when it is cool to tuck in a few leftover seeds here and there in blank and shady spots in the garden. Seed packets usually give the number of days to maturity, and seed catalogues always do. There are 60 days from now to mid-September, and cool-weather crops, like lettuce, beets, carrots, broccoli, and spinach will continue to grow here on Block Island into November. But, some of these, lettuce and spinach especially, do not germinate well in hot weather, so will do better if started a bit later, perhaps in mid-August.

Last December I dug twenty carrots, planted in July, from a raised bed with a heavy hay mulch, for Christmas dinner. They were eight inches long, sweet, thick, and delicious. Carrots are easy to grow, the secret being in the planting, especially the soil preparation. They must be able to grow straight down without interference from stones or hard pan. Who wants two-legged carrots? I dig several trenches, break up the soil at the bottom, half fill with compost, and stamp down. Nice pulverized soil goes on top, then the seed planted and lightly covered. Radish seeds planted about every two inches will come up first and keep the soil from crusting, so that the little carrot seeds can come through. When the carrots are up, pull out the radishes, which have served their purpose. Carrots should be thinned to grow two to four inches apart, depending on the variety. I eliminate this step by using pelleted seed (from Harris), little beads that are easy to plant at the proper spacing. There is still plenty of time to plant carrots for fall and winter harvest. If mulched heavily later on so that the ground doesn't freeze, they may be dug all winter. This spring I found two that I had missed last winter, and cooked them for dinner. Delicious!

Gardening is such an imprecise and variable activity that there is never a dull moment. It is full of surprises, pleasant and otherwise, and can also be baffling at times. I get many calls from my friends with problems and, of course, am unable to solve lots of them. Sometimes the answer is simply, "Bad luck!" At present I have a very kind friend who has just retired and taken up gardening. He is an engineer with a logical trained mind, believing that two and two always make four. It isn't easy to convince him that sometimes they make zero, and occasionally ten, like my two spring carrots.

Tomatoes

Perhaps our consuming worry now is our tomato crop, doing fine until a hot dry season comes along. If you see black or brown spots on the bottom of your tomatoes, you have that fearsome pest "blossom end rot", and there is no cure for it. Pick off affected fruit and toss it out. Staked plants which have been heavily pruned seem to be hit first, and really the only way to avoid the problem is to expect it, to mulch and water thoroughly and often. A good supply of calcium in the soil seems to be helpful. Mix a tablespoonful of calcium chloride (road salt) in a pint of water and pour around the base of each plant. Don't ever remove foliage to hasten ripening, as tomatoes, like humans, need protection from the hot sun. I have found some affected tomatoes near the top of my plants, grown in cages and very large, but the ones underneath, being nearer to moisture and shaded heavily, seem to be okay. My fingers are crossed! If your plants are grown unstaked, put plenty of clean straw or hay underneath them to prevent the fruit from rotting.

Tomatoes should be heavily mulched to conserve the moisture, but even more importantly to prevent soil splashing up on the foliage, causing the leaves to turn brown. Start dusting them now with BT to prevent those nasty, little fruit worms, who make small holes in the fruit and then crawl inside for shelter and continuing sustenance.

Eat the Flowers

Salad days are here, with lettuce and radishes at their best. For variety, try a few other additions: weeds and flowers. Did you know that purslane contains several cancer-fighting substances, as well as being loaded with vitamin C and beta-carotene? It tastes a bit like spinach, to which it is related, and may be eaten cooked or raw. Chicory leaves, cress, dandelion, and lamb's quarters are all edible and good for you, and of course nasturtiums add zing and beauty to any salad. Weeds should be picked young before they become bitter. The blossoms of nasturtiums have a peppery taste, and may be kept fresh in a plastic bag, refrigerated, for several days, but use the leaves and stems at once before they wilt.

The best way to dry parsley for future use is to wash it, pat it dry with paper toweling, and place it in a brown paper bag in the refrigerator until it is dry. Then store it in a clean, airtight glass jar.

The mosquitoes have arrived, also biting flies, especially annoying early and late in the day. Remember that mosquitoes breed in standing water. In Florida, where I lived for fifteen winters, everyone had a rain barrel attached to a downspout, and I have one here too. The mosquito-breeding problem can be solved by three or four drops of kerosene on the surface of the water, which spread out and kill the larvae.

Houseplants

This is an ideal time to repot your houseplants and a cool spot for this activity can usually be found in the garage, or even outside, if you have a shady area under a nice big tree, which catches the southwest breeze. Potting soil, already mixed, is available at most garden supply centers, but it is expensive, and it is so easy to make your own. The simple formula is one-third soil, one-third humus, and one-third coarse sand. All you need to prepare this mixture is a quarter-inch mesh soil sifter and a wheelbarrow. I use the soil from my vegetable garden, rotted compost, and builder's sand (not beach sand, which is too salty). Perlite may be substituted for sand...it is almost weightless...or the two mixed together. Add a handful or two of bonemeal, and a little dehydrated cow manure if you have it, but avoid other fertilizer until the plants are growing happily in their new home.

We are advised by the experts to move our houseplants outdoors for the summer, probably a good idea if you have a cool, shady, moist spot near the house, which I do not. I really see no reason for doing this anyway. My big, south bay window gets limited sunlight during July and August, the back door nearby is always open, windows too, and I like having my plants near me. After all, they are old friends and, like the dogs, need daily doses of care and love.

Choices

One of the many garden publications I take recently asked its subscribers to name their five favorite perennials. We all have our choices, plants that grow well for us, and speak to us in a special way. My criteria are beauty, hardiness, neatness, and ease of culture, and my final vote was for iris, columbine, summer phlox, chrysanthemum, and dictamnus. This last is a plant not familiar to everyone. It should be used as an accent in the border, given plenty of room, and never moved. It will outlive your descendants! It grows two to three feet tall, never needs staking, and is insect free. The rather unattractive common name of this marvel is gas plant, also sometimes referred to as burning bush, and for a good reason. The stalks and leaves give off a volatile lemon-scented oil, and on a windless, hot, July night a lighted match at the base of the plant produces a spectacular flash of light as the oil ignites, with no harm whatsoever to the plant. When our children were growing up, a frequent question was, "When can we light the gas plant?" an event they have never forgotten. Unfortunately, these plants are hard to find. The one I have here came from White Flower Farm in Litchfield, CT. It is two years old, and has three beautiful, pink spikes in bloom this year. Next year it will be big enough to light! The seedpods are perfection for dried arrangements.

Dividing Iris

One of the loveliest and most faithful denizens of our northeast gardens is the bearded iris, cultivated by the Chinese long before the birth of Christ. Iris are so easy to grow that we tend to treat them with undeserved neglect while we hover over fussier plants. They will survive somehow in poor soil, surrounded by weeds, and even shaded by taller companions, but you will be amazed by the show of beauty they will give if treated like honored and loved friends.

Iris should be divided and replanted every three or four years, depending on how close together they were planted initially, and from now until mid-August is the time to do so. Later allows them too little time to develop new anchoring roots, and they will tend to heave out with winter frosts. So equip yourself with a spading fork, a pair of sharp shears, a good kitchen knife, and perhaps a knee pad!

Dig up the old clumps, shake them free of soil, and cut off the strong outside divisions, making sure they have some live roots. Discard the old worn-out centers. Trim the leaves with shears on a slant about four inches above the rhizome and prune the roots to the same length. Examine the rhizome carefully for brown spots indicating rot, usually caused by iris borers, cut to clean fiber, and expose to sunlight to callous the cut. It is wise to air all new divisions for several days, washing them off first in a solution of one part Clorox to eight parts water, and then dusting the cuts with sulpher before planting.

Iris are not fussy about soil, as long as it is welldrained, not acid, and in full sun. A pH 6 to 8 is fine. As all perennials do, they thrive on light fertilizing, both when replanted and after blooming, but avoid heavy manure. Compost or dehydrated cow manure is fine if dug down eight inches deep, and bonemeal is always acceptable. Set the plants in a triangle of three or five, about a foot apart, with the fans facing the same way. If you have room to set them eighteen inches apart, they won't have to be divided again quite so soon. Make two openings in the soil about an inch apart, slanting away from each other, and place the rhizome firmly on the saddle with roots extending down on either side, thus eliminating an air pocket under the rhizome, the top of which should be exposed to the sunlight. Firm and water thoroughly.

The irises in so many of our gardens have been there for a long time. Where did they come from? Who gave them to us? Most of them are blue or "fried egg" yellow with a few dark maroon shades. If you have never grown the west coast hybrids, you are missing a garden delight. These stately irises come in every color of the rainbow, the flowers are huge and ruffled, and the sturdy stalks need no staking. Even the names of them are intriguing: China Dragon, Grand Waltz, Gypsy Caravan, and Columbia Blue, the finest tall blue iris I've ever seen. These are old varieties, long time friends of mine. New iris hybrids can cost as much as $45 and more each, but most breeders offer collections that are moderately priced, all fine varieties and many of them award winners from previous years. Mine came from Schreiner's in Oregon, where at present you can order eight divisions for about $42, or, less than the price of a good dinner at a Block Island eatery! Cooley is another fine source with a beautiful catalogue that will leave you day-. dreaming. Both these growers ship in August and early September, so some protection is advisable for the first winter.

Biennials

Now that the display of spring bulbs and iris is past, and the annuals have not yet reached their top performance, the flower beds seem to be mostly green. The answer to this problem is biennials, flowers that are produced by plants grown the previous year, and this is the time to order seed and start them, so that next year you will have their lovely display — and for many years after as they self-sow freely and keep the timetable going. My favorites are foxglove (*Digitalis*), sweet william, hollyhocks, and pansies, which bloom all winter in my garden and seed everywhere.

Many people seem to have the erroneous impression that a biennial is a plant that blooms every two years, when actually it is a plant designed by nature to live for one year only. It is grown from seed one year, blooms the following spring, then dies. This is true of Canterbury bells, but sweet william and foxglove self-sow very freely, as do pansies, and the original sweet william plants often live for many years. Anyway, they are such satisfactory garden additions, and so easy to grow — who would be without them? They fill the gap between the spring bloom in the garden and the later show put on by annuals and summer-blooming perennials, and if once planted will usually persist through their seedlings.

Seeds started now will grow into sturdy plants by late August and may then be moved to their permanent locations, where the cool autumn weather will help them to establish deep roots. They may be started indoors, in a cold frame, or in a shady, protected spot in the vegetable garden, kept moist until they germinate, and perhaps further protected by floating Reemay cloth. When planting them, just sprinkle sifted soil very lightly over the area, remembering that the mature plants self-sow with no cover at all.

Don't be in a hurry to cut off the spent seedpods of biennials. The plants look shabby, but if left to their own devices will drop their seeds and provide a wealth of little plants to be moved to new homes in early fall. I always have pansies, sweet william, foxglove, and hollyhocks in my gardens, gifts from nature, and of course lunaria, also called honesty or money plant, one of my favorites. It is grown primarily for its seed pods, sprays of silvery coins to be used dry all winter, but the spring bloom, a brilliant, cool pinky purple, is a lovely bonus. It does best in a partly shady spot. This year I had a surprise display over my wall where I had dumped a bucket of weeds last summer.

Pansies

Pansies are beloved by all gardeners, and there are few gardens indeed where the spring scene is not enhanced by these cheerful little plants. Years ago, like many of us today, I had always bought a few baskets of them at the local hardware store, and tucked them into the front of the border, where they put on a brave show until the hot, dry summer put an end to it. Then one year I went to visit a friend in Brooklin, Maine, in mid-July. There in his garden I saw pansies that made me gasp, bushy plants with flowers three inches across, and bowls of blossoms on all the tables in the house. He sent me some of his excess seed in August, and since that time I have grown my own pansies every other year. Of course the cool nights and moist air of the Maine coast are ideal for pansies, but even where the summers are hot and dry, home-grown pansies will stand the heat and will produce blossoms of a size and color never found in those from a supermarket. Seed should be ordered in July, and bear in mind that good seed is expensive. The plants bearing the finest and most unusual blossoms are generally poor seed producers. The cost of this top quality seed puts it beyond the reach of some commercial growers, but to the home gardener, the additional cost is negligible. Park Seed has a fine collection of pansy seed, including Majestic Giants hybrids with flowers four inches across, and my favorite, Imperial Antique shades, three-inch flowers in lovely, pale colors with ruffled edges. The cost is $2.75 for a packet of twenty-five seeds, but the germination is excellent. Where could you find such plants for 11¢ apiece? If happy in your garden, they will self-sow and you will have pansies for many years, as they know how and when to plant themselves!

Dog Days

The long, hot days of summer are with us here, for most of July and half of August, a period often referred to as the dog days, a time of year the ancients believed drove men and dogs to madness. Of course our dogs always need our loving care, summer and winter, but the name dog days really refers to the star Sirius, its name derived from a Greek word meaning "brilliant, or scorching." Sirius is the brightest star in the heavens, and the best known after Polaris. It is the chief star in the constellation of the Greater Dog.

In our latitudes Sirius is really a winter star that follows the path of the sun, to be first seen in mid-November when the sun sets early. It blazes low in the southern sky just to the left of Orion. *Bullfinch's Mythology* recounts the charming tale of Diana's accidental shooting of Orion, whereupon "she placed him among the stars where he appears as a giant with a girdle, sword, lion's skin and club. Sirius, his dog, follows him [just as a good dog should], and the Pleiades, Diana's nymphs, fly before him."

Last night I woke at 2 a.m. and went out on my deck to look at the stars. The ocean was voicing its soft rhythms in the distance, a bullfrog was saying what bullfrogs say in a nearby pond, and the Milky Way was a beautiful scarf of light across the sky above me. We take the stars for granted, but I often wonder how we would feel about them if we saw this miracle only every ten or twenty years, like eclipses and comets.

Hic, Haec, Hoc

Latin and Greek are no longer required subjects in most schools, but nature can take over as a fine teacher if we gardeners pay attention to the names of our birds, garden plants, stars, and the signs of the zodiac, even the clouds. Our white flowers have *alba* added to their names, as red ones have *rubra*. The mocking-bird is *Mimus polyglottos* (many-tongued mimic), the tree sparrow has *arborea* attached to his name, and the white-throated sparrow has *alba collis* (white collar) added. The little songsparrow's full name is *Melospiza melodia*, which sounds just like its song. The word *cumulus* suggests clouds piled up like whipped cream, the *equinox* (equal night) and *solstice* (sun stand still) are both Latin words, as is the *equator* (equal) where the days and nights are always the same length.

Learning the scientific names of the outdoor world around us brings many pleasant surprises, and it is amusing to think of those ancient (to us) Romans, sashaying around in their togas and sandals, using the same words that we nature lovers do to communicate with each other.

And how useful this knowledge can sometimes be! My pansy-growing friend in Maine also grows fancy blueberries, believed by natives and tourist alike to be free for the picking. He erected several signs around the field reading "*Vaccinium Corymbosum* has been found on these premises!" He loses only a few berries to the birds, who either understand Latin or can't read!

Bye-Bye, July

I sometimes wonder what it is that defines the difference between work and play. We say "play tennis or golf, but work in the garden. For me, an afternoon in the garden watering, weeding, listening to the birds with the warm sun on my back, and outwitting my little dog who is trying to sneak through the gate, is a time of relaxation and play of the highest order, without striving for perfection or trying to be better than someone else. Perhaps it is age that changes one's attitude, an added plus to being slightly "old." We must learn to be more laid-back about everything, and this summer has been a test of progress for me, what with the drought (being broken as I write this), a bout with Lyme disease, and a sprained wrist from too much weeding, which my neighbor tells me is carpal tunnel syndrome, an ailment caused by overuse of computers, an occult activity with which I am unfamiliar.

To preserve the high tone of these July observations, which started with Shakespeare, let us close with the Bible: "And let us not be weary in well doing: for in due season we shall reap, if we faint not. (Gal. 6:9 AV)."

August

The world puts on its robes of glory now;
The very flowers are tinged with deeper dyes;
The waves are bluer, and the angels pitch
Their shining tents along the sunset skies.
       — Albert Leighton

August is high on my list of favorite months. All that spring labor now seems to be rewarding us with fresh veggies to eat, flowers of "deeper hues" to pick and to enjoy in our gardens, and light evenings when it is cool outside and we can even do a little gardening here and there. The monthlong July drought discouraged weed growth, and the recent rainfall has helped our flower gardens put on their "robes of glory."

Last Sunday's downpour registered one-and-a-half inches on my big rain gauge, and seemed like a true gift from Heaven, not only for the gardens and lawns on the Island, but also I suspect for the many summer visitors, who must be weary of cross, sunburnt children, dust, and unbearable heat. Everyone seemed to look happier on Monday. As John Burroughs wrote, "I think rain is as necessary to the mind as to vegetation. My own thoughts become thirsty, and crave the moisture."

And was it Mark Twain who said, "Everyone talks about the weather, but nobody does anything about it"? Here on Block Island, it is impossible to estimate how many comments on the weather surface in a single day, and this summer, especially, it has been an engrossing topic: the late spring, the dry month of June, the foggy weekends, the hot and dry August, and, of course, our good luck so far in escaping hurricanes! It seems at times that the great American public resents any weather that interferes with its playtime. The skiers long for deep snow, which causes misery to the city dwellers; the sailors hope for wind, which can ruin the fishing; and even the weather in Florida, the land of endless sunshine, was a disappointment to many last winter, cooler than usual with periods of gray, overcast skies.

But weather has been going on for a long time, and as every gardener and farmer knows, it is unpredictable and not to be controlled by mortals. When storms and disaster hover nearby, those close to the land are better able to "keep their cool," trusting in the gods above rather than in the electric company to pull them through. Perhaps the fact that most gardeners are optimists gives them a psychological advantage. They expect good things to happen, but are accepting of the opposite, knowing that "bad things can happen to good gardeners." And then, there is always next year and probably better luck.

As Ye Plant So Shall Ye Reap

Now the summer is nearly over, Labor Day not far off, and our gardens releasing their bounty, almost too much of it in some areas. It seems to come all at once, and hating waste after all our labor, we harvest, freeze, can tomato juice, and make sure that our neighbors have their share of our largesse. Swapping veggies is fun. I always have lots of cucumbers, eggplant, peppers, and beans, but one year had no zucchini, and was then owned by a fifteen-year-old dachshund who loved it, raw. My neighbors kindly kept him supplied. (Till we meet again, dear Freddy!)

My first concern just now is the big vegetable garden, always an ongoing project, and I know those weeds are in there, waiting to get revenge for any neglect, as they steal moisture and nutrients from our crops.

My peppers and eggplant are grown together, sharing a different bed every year. Peppers may be harvested at several stages, according to the size and color you like. They produce only a certain number of fruits at one time, and will then stop blossoming until some of the peppers are picked, when flowers will reappear. Both peppers and eggplant will benefit from an Epsom Salts spray on the blossoms, one teaspoonful in a one ounce spray bottle.

Spuds

Potatoes may be harvested as "new" (immature), ready to eat when they reach golf-ball size, or dug as mature when the tops die down. In June I planted ten marble-sized Desiree potatoes. The soil had been lowered to a pH 5 by addition of copper sulfate, the growing plants were kept watered and mulched, and yesterday I dug eight pounds of potatoes with no sign of scab or other imperfections, and of course no chemicals to make the skins inedible. They will be stored in an airy spot in the garage with newspaper cover to keep out the light.

If you are presently feeling bored by white potatoes, cheer up. Blue, pink, and yellow potatoes are now making their way to the vegatable garden, and the ratings for flavor and keeping-quality are very high, plus a slightly higher mineral content than the usual brown and white spuds. My *Garden Sampler* newsletter lists some intriguing varieties, i.e., Ruby Crescent (pink skin and yellow flesh), Yellow Fingerling, Peruvian Blue (dark purple flesh with white ring, and dark blue skin), and Russian Banana, a yellow that looks "buttery." And there is All Blue, which is truly blue, both skin and flesh. Other than blueberries and plums I can't think of many other blue foods, blue crabs and bluefish perhaps, and my curiosity will prompt me to try one or two of these potatoes next spring.

I read recently that potatoes do not thrive in compost-rich soil, which proves to me that even plants have some strange tastes. The bed is now sown to a buckwheat covercrop, to be pulled up later for the compost bin, rather than being dug under.

And speaking of potatoes, *The Avant Gardener,* says that they should always be peeled before cooking, as the peels of purchased spuds almost always contain residues of a sprout inhibitor, which has proved toxic in animal tests, and even homegrown potatoes contain natural toxins in their skins that can move into the flesh while boiling, but less during baking. Like most of us, I have eaten potato skins all my life, and shall continue to do so in spite of this dire warning!

Onions

Onions should be harvested as soon as the tops start to wither, and the drier they are, the better they will store. Bend over the tops with the back of a rake, and let them sit for a day or two. Then loosen and pull up carefully, leaving them bottom-side up on the bed until the roots are dry and break off easily. They should be cured for two weeks or so in a warm, airy place in the shade. I spread them out in those plastic open-lattice seed flats, set on square milk boxes in my open shed or garage. Turn them several times to promote even drying, then sort by size and hang in a mesh bag in the garage, or store in a root cellar, if you are lucky enough to have one. Never cut off any green tops, as rot will surely start there and ruin the crop.

There is still time to plant beets and carrots, so welcome when the beans are petering out and an early frost signals summer's end. Remember that carrots may be harvested all winter if covered with a thick mulch of hay or straw. I suspect the same is true of beets. Lettuce is a fast crop, 64 days fom seeding to maturity, and may be enjoyed all fall at its very best. So take a little time to clear a weedy area for these undemanding crops.

There are some simple techniques to keep short-term crops producing far beyond their normal season. Of course beans and cucumbers must be kept picked, remembering that once seed is set, plants have done their job. You can make beans bear into autumn by cutting the old leaves away, starting at the bottom where they first mature, and gradually moving up. New foliage and flowers, and a good late crop of beans will come along. The same procedure works with squash and cukes. Tomato plants can be topped off to stop new growth, which cannot produce fruit before frost. If you root-prune a plant or two, it will hasten ripening of fruit. Take a spade or knife and cut down around half the plant six to eight inches deep at a distance of six inches from the base. This is scary to do, but it works. The plant is stressed by this and hurries to produce seed. Who says plants don't feel and think?

The burning daily question is, "What shall we have for dinner?" Freshly pulled beets, little, crisp string beans, tiny new carrots, eggplant dipped in beaten egg, Italian bread crumbs lightly sauteed, or salad with cucumbers and tomatoes as sweet as ripe fruit? I cook most of my fresh vegetables in a Presto pressure cooker, with one-half cup of water (ten minutes for beets, two minutes for beans, et cetera.). This cooker is sixty years old and built to last forever. About every two years I write to the company in Eau Claire, WI, for a new safety valve and a couple of sealing rings, "One size fits all."

Weeding

> Oh, Adam was a gardener,
> And God who made him sees
> That half a proper gardener's work
> Is done upon his knees.
> — Rudyard Kipling

It isn't easy to gear ourselves up for the attack this late in the gardening year, but leaving weeds to flourish now is almost a guarantee of a miserable spring to come, as this fall is really the start of next year's growing season. Many of our weeds are perennial and will develop deep root systems if left alone. Some grasses grow by underground stolons, and if left to spread will make a mat deep in the soil, almost impossible to dig out. And in the spring the soil is cold and wet, and trampling it can do serious damange. Lastly, we are all in better physical shape now than we will be after a long, housebound winter!

Weeds love nice, empty areas where crops have flourished, so before they can start, sow some cover crop over these sections. I use buckwheat, which should be turned under before frost. It grows fast, is not invasive, adds nitrogen, and the white flowers are beloved by bees. Our gardens do not grow feeble with age as we do, but improve as we care for them. With a little help from us now, next spring will find them as youthful and energetic as a teenager. So, as our modern savants would probably say, "Continue to eliminate the undesirable herbage."

Drought

> My beets and carrots were planted late,
> And showed no urge to germinate.

The drought is with us still, and yet
Perhaps some day it will be WET.
   — JBF

August is a time for the gardener to "hang in there" and take it easy. Today there is an east wind, cool and gentle, not like the battering gales we so dread in the winter. It is a welcome relief from the heat, but sad to say brings no rain, and the soil four inches down is powder dry. We cannot water everything, but there are priorities to be bravely met.

Our first concern should be for our trees and shrubs, and only deep watering is effective for them. They will tell you when they are stressed by either wilting or dropping their leaves. This is a defense mechanism, as plants take up moisture from the soil and release it into the air through their leaves, a process they simply close down when there is no moisture to be had. And they go deep for it, so you must go deep too, by letting a hose or soil soaker drip slowly for two or three hours.

Our perennials come next, the special denizens of our gardens, acquired after much pouring through catalogues, and lots of TLC upon arrival. Don't neglect them, and don't move or divide them now.

Lawns take a lot of water, but seem to survive somehow without it, and usually come back to green health when the rain finally comes. Needless to say, don't fertilize anything until the drought breaks. After all, we don't feed big meals to people who are gasping for breath.

I read in today's *New York Times* that a new type of virus is loose, attacking everyone's computers. My grandchildren must be worried! As for me, I am happy in the realization that my faithful Smith Corona is immune to most such horrors, with the possible exception of an easily replaced worn-out ribbon. Besides, we gardeners have plenty of other matters to concern us.

August Seeds

My new pansy seed, ordered ten days ago, is lying on the table here, awaiting August planting. The seed may be sown in shallow seed flats, a cold frame, or a protected spot in the garden, in good soil with some humus added to retain moisture. Sow it thinly, and cover with about one-eighth of sifted soil or sand. The seed must be kept shaded and moist until it germinates. Flats may be kept in the shade of a porch, or if seed is sown in a cold frame it may be covered with lath to which burlap is fastened. I use an old window screen with Reemay covering. The frequency of watering will depend on the weather, but under no circumstances let the seed become dry, as germination moisture is the most important single requirement for good results. Use a fine spray, a rubber bulb perhaps, so as not to wash out the seed. There is absolutely no point in sowing pansy seed and leaving for a week's vacation. You would do better to bury the money you paid for the seed — at least you could dig that up on your return.

Germination usually takes about two weeks, although some of the finer varieties take a little longer. Do not be discouraged if germination appears to be poor at first, as the seed will continue to sprout for ten days or so after the first speck of green has appeared. As soon as the seed has started to germinate, remove the burlap, but keep the tiny plants lightly shaded with lath or a screen. Moisture is still important; a whole planting may be lost by one day's neglect. When several true leaves have appeared, your pansies are ready for a new home. They may be transplanted into six packs, small pots, or tucked into the cold frame several inches apart, and after several weeks more lined out in a spare vegetable bed. When the ground freezes, give them a light mulch of salt hay or Reemay cloth. They will winter there happily, and will be ready to dig and plant into your spring gardens.

There are other garden flowers whose seed is winter hardy, and they may be started now for transplanting to the borders early next spring. Larkspur, and bachelor's buttons come to mind, also some poppies, and I have had very good luck in the past with sweet william, lunaria, foxgloves, and even snapdragons. A cold frame is the perfect spot for this, but any protected corner or nook in the vegetable garden will yield good results.

My gardening neighbor, John Hobe, tells me that Block Island's climate really belongs to zone 8, not zone 6, and my experience so far indicates that he is correct in this, as in many other matters.

Delphiniums

Everyone loves delphiniums and no wonder; they are the most beautiful and majestic denizens of the flower garden! Up in Maine where the winters are long and cold, with no March thaws they are true perennials, but the mild and varied winters here often produce crown rot, and if not, the hot humid days of summer will finish them off. Here they should be treated as biennials, started in late summer or early fall, the seed bought in August as it must be fresh to germinate, and given some protection over the winter.

August Chores

Recently I have been taking my own advice and cutting back petunias, a sticky job I dislike. Where does one stop? In fact I always feel weary of petunias by August 1. Everyone has them and they are always the same, but their bright colors create a bonanza for growers in the spring when we all long for instant flowers. In Florida, where I spent fifteen winters, the ubiquitous hibiscus serves a similar purpose.

Petunias offer very little challenge to the adventurous gardener, but there are other annuals that require patience and an ever trustful frame of mind. This year I grew godetia, started from seed on March 21, under grow lights. It is now in bloom in a raised bed in the vegetable garden and is absolutely gorgeous, low growing with masses of one-and-a-half cups in luscious colors: watermelon pinks, vivid reds, white with pink throats, pale pinks, apricots, and many variations.

Staking

Late-blooming perennials should be staked in early August before the rains and high winds of fall flatten them to the ground. Everyone has his own mode of staking, and if the result is obvious the method is poor. So don't gather your plants into tight bunches tied up to broomsticks. A good system for large clumps is to place three or four stakes around the plant and pass string back and forth through it. For some plants you will need individual thin sticks for each spike. The idea is to keep the natural shape of the plant intact. Green string and stakes are the least obvious. Support for dahlias should be set before planting, to avoid damage to the tubers when staking.

Peonies & Poppies

Recently I have had several inquiries about moving and dividing peonies and oriental poppies, and am at a loss to understand why anyone would feel the urge to do so. These are both perennials that put down deep roots, improve with age, and resent being disturbed. However, if they must be moved to another location, August or early September is the time. Peonies should be replanted with the eyes not more than two inches belowground, or they will not bloom, and as they are heavy feeders, they require deep and thorough soil preparation.

Poppies present another problem: If there is an inch or less of old root left in the ground, a new plant will appear next spring — in fact, nurserymen propagate them by planting three-inch pieces of the old root in pots and growing them in a cold frame over the winter. The main disadvantage of these lovely orientals is that they gradually disappear after blooming, leaving a rather large bare area in the border, but a clump of baby's breath or hardy asters planted nearby, but not too close, makes a good fill-in. Although their spring blooming period is rather short, the sight is so breathtakingly gorgeous that other drawbacks seem irrelevant. Most gardeners find it unnecessary to mark their location, as it is not easily forgotten. The new crowns usually appear in September.

As poppies go dormant after blooming and disappear, label them now so that you won't plant something else in the empty space, this also applies to platycodon and butterfly weed, which come up very late in spring. Feed chrysanthemums to encourage good bloom. Any handy garden fertilizer may be sprinkled in a ring around the plants, and watered in. If you plan to put daffodils in the garden later, leave space at the back of the beds, so that the other plants will hide the unsightly ripening foliage.

Odds & Ends

Are you up-to-date on the latest garden tools? Recently, *Organic Gardening* featured a six-page article on ten different hoes and *Horticulture* discussed string trimmers, listing seventy models ranging in price from $25 to $700. Power equipment is a must today for big areas, but remember that it causes air and noise pollution, and, like our cars, demands regular maintenance service. Two years ago I bought a reel mower from Smith and Hawken and have found it a great help for quick touch-ups here and there, even for mowing around my vegetable garden where the grass grows fast and thick. The modern reel mowers weigh as little as nineteen pounds, seldom need sharpening, and give a lovely, smooth, even cut. They are easy to push, and provide pleasant exercise and the nostalgic sound of bygone days.

This is a fine time to clean out your birdhouses and feeders and to dust the inside of the houses with rotenone or BT to kill any parasites. I am still feeding the goldfinches as they begin nesting in July or early August when most other birds are coping with their kids, and locate their nests near stands of thistle seed, their favorite food and their choice for the nestlings too. This is really a year-round handout for me, but I can't imagine not having those gay, bright friends on my feeder and in the birdbath every evening.

Did you know that the monarch butterfly is our national insect? I was unaware of this earth-shaking fact until I ran across a comment in *The Avant Gardener* (a leaflet I peruse with pleasure and interest) to the effect that the lightning bug is being proposed as an alternate candidate by the *Southern Farmer's Almanac*, their reason being that it is more familiar to the majority of Americans!

Good news gleanings from my readings: The Beagle Brigade, a group of fifty, are on duty at our international airports, trained to sniff out hidden plant, animal, and food products that carry pests or diseases; a four-leaf clover is found in nature on only one plant in a thousand, but the University of Florida has genetically produced plants with completely four-leaved foliage, insuring plenty of good luck for all of us!

Late August

The weary August days are long:
The locusts sing a plaintive song,
The cattle miss their master's call
When they see the sunset shadows fall.
      — E.C. Stedman

Sometimes when I wake at night in the dark, the rasping sound of the cicadas tells me that the autumn is drawing near, just as the peepers in the spring tell us of summer joys to come. To me, the song of the cicadas and katydids is comforting, telling of restful times ahead, the curtains drawn, lights on a little earlier, and cosy, pleasant hours indoors with books, music, and pursuits other than the garden. As for the cattle, I am fortunate in having John Littlefield's meadows between my land and the sea, and frequently the lovely sight of his brown and white cows grazing nearby.

We have had ample rainfall at last, and what a difference it has made in our gardens! They are full of color: impatiens, marigolds, zinnias, alyssum, snapdragons, everything perked up and looking happy, as I feel too. Volunteers are everywhere, pansies in the garden paths, petunias in the onion bed, and a large clump of alyssum in bloom in my lily-of-the-valley bed, at least thirty feet away from any other plant. How did it get there?

A Poem Lovely as a Tree

It is sad to see the dead and dying pines all over the Island, and expensive to take them down and remove them or have them converted to mulch. I have none here, but the adjacent properties are full of them, and no prospect of removal. If all these dead trees would just disappear, it would open up the lovely vistas well remembered from my childhood, so many years ago. Fortunately, I am screened near the house by two maples and an oak, planted six years ago for privacy. At that time I also planted a maple off the southwest corner of the house to give some protection from the hot afternoon sun. This tree has provided me with a nice, shady garden area, my only one, wrapped around the corner of the house foundation. This spring I raised some caladiums for the first time, and am now enjoying their huge spectacular multicolored leaves. This little garden is three feet wide, and about eighteen feet long, and besides the caladiums is planted with astilbes, several choice daylillies, and a border of coleus and double impatiens, all doing well thanks to my maple.

> Flowers are lovely; love is flower like;
> Friendship is a sheltering tree.
> —Samuel Coleridge

September

The day is cold and dark and dreary,
It rains and the wind is never weary;
The vine still clings to the mouldering wall,
And with every gust the dead leaves fall,
And the day is dark and dreary.
        - Henry Wadsworth Longfellow

Such dismal lines from a usually cheerful poet! Today, it is gray and drizzly out, with rain forecast for the rest of the week. September always seems a sad month to me, a combination perhaps of summer being over, early dusk, equinoctial storms, wedges of geese heading south, and a general letdown of gardening energy and enthusiasm. But our annuals are a blaze of color, chrysanthemums are finally in bloom, the wild places loaded with berries, flowers, and autumn hues. And soon to come is "October's bright blue weather," always a special time on Block Island.

The full moon we have just enjoyed in the clear night skies is the harvest moon, the name given to the full moon nearest the autumnal equinox, September 21. The pundits say that a warm week preceding this date foretells a mild winter. I tend to believe what the woolly bears tell us, but so far have not been advised. It is a matter-of-fact, however, that at present the length of our daylight and the position of the sun are the same as in late March, since we are now three months past the summer solstice. These lovely, windless, warm days make that really hard to believe.

Lawns

The present is a perfect time to turn our attention to our usually neglected lawns. Mine is always weedy and poor in the important areas, and lush and green in the out-of-the-way places. It has been a great year for dandelions and crabgrass, but I am happy to inform you that Gardens Alive has a new product that promises help. (All their products are organic and safe.) This is called A-Mazing Lawn, and is a by-product of corn syrup production. It is used in pet foods and chicken feed, so it presents no danger to children, pets, or to chickens either, of course! It acts as a preemergent weed control, which stops dandelions, crabgrass, and many other weeds by killing their new, little feeder roots. It should be used now as weeds are seeding and again next spring. A fifty-pound bag covers twenty-five-hundred square feet fifty-by-fifty feet and costs about $40, less of course if you buy several bags. If in addition you apply lime and organic fertilizer now, you should see happy improvements next spring, when most of us are too busy to worry about grass! Gardens Alive offers many other organic products and garden aids, as well as fine problem-solving advice. Do send for their catalogues.

Weeds

I will go root away
The noisome weeds which without profit suck
The soil's fertility from wholesome flowers.
   —William Shakespeare

"Weed" has graced the top of my morning "To Do" list for most of the summer so far, but at present everything seems to be under control, except for a few areas in the flower beds, to be taken care of before next week, when the Garden Club descends on me expecting, I'm afraid, to see perfection, for how else can they trust my advice?

There are times when I wonder why anyone has a garden, an endless source of frustration, worry, and hard work. Of course, the answers are myriad. If started, there is no end to it. The garden becomes a possession, like a house, needing cleaning, defense from marauders, beautification, and ongoing love and concern. But unlike houses, our gardens are always changing and teaching us. If we have ears to listen, they talk to us of success and failure, present us with new discoveries and surprises, forgive us for neglect. They add untold pleasure and excitement to the "dailiness" of living, pat us on the back for attention, and flatter our egos, even convincing me at times that I'm not old! The net of all this is that I am a sucker for nature, both flora and fauna, with special emphasis on the canine variety of the latter.

Recently I spotted a lovely vine growing up the new railings at our Harbor Church, and fortunately realized that it was bittersweet, an interloper of the most invasive intent. How did it get there? John Burroughs once wrote, "Weeds are great travelers; they are indeed the tramps of the vegetable world. They go east, west, north, south; they walk, they play, they swim, they steal a ride, they travel by rails, by flood, by wind; they go underground, they go above, across lots, and by highways."

Here on Block Island we enjoy the beauty of many weeds along our roadsides against our gray stone walls, and in our meadows, but not in our gardens; and this year's strange summer has produced a record influx. The late, cool spring covered my garden with chickweed, the seeds of which are now sprouting everywhere, along with huge mats of crabgrass, all of which must be dealt with. Weeds love nice, empty areas where crops have flourished, so before they can start, sow some cover crop over these sections, or protect them with landscape cloth.

Seeds

Seeds, like everything else nowadays, are becoming more expensive, and the packets smaller. I recently paid $1.95 for a packet of 25 pansy seeds, but these are antique pastel shades with ruffled edges, so we must consider the years of selective breeding involved before these little gems could be offered for sale. Some years ago, Burpee offered a large money prize for a white marigold, although why anyone would want one I couldn't imagine. This offer stood for many years, and they now do offer a white marigold called French Vanilla, fully double, creamywhite blossoms on two-foot tall plants. Seed price is $4.25 (50 seeds) and worth every penny. Plants are also available.

The temptation is to save seeds from our own plants, even to beg some from our friends who have flowers we would like to grow in our gardens, but over the years I have found that such seed germinates poorly, does not come true to color or size, and in general produces such disappointing results that it is not worth the effort. And the work of growing our own plants from seed is considerable!

But saving leftover seed that we have paid for is a different matter altogether, and can save us considerable expense, especially in the area of the vegetable garden. According to the *National Geographic* (a very back issue), when King Tut's tomb was opened in Egypt, in addition to the fabulous gems and gold artifacts, bean seeds were found, which still germinated. My bean seed packets are left lying around in my garden shed most of the summer, a far cry from the preservation methods of ancient Egypt, but this year I bought no new bean seed, and had fine germination from the old. The ideal way to store leftover seed is to provide low temperature and low humidity, so tuck them into a tightly closed glass jar on a back shelf of the fridge during the spring and summer, and keep them in an unheated garage through the fall and winter. A good sprinkling of freshly opened powdered milk in the bottom of each jar will insure that the seeds stay dry. With this treatment you may expect the following results: two years viability for carrots, onions, and corn; three years for peas, beans, peppers, radishes, and beets; four years for cucumbers, melons, lettuce, broccoli, cabbage, and squash.

Marigold seed will keep for several years with no babying at all; in fact, I save all kinds of flower seeds too, as there is an easy way to test them for germination in the spring, by placing a few seeds between two layers of damp paper towels in a warm spot for a week or two. If more than half begin to sprout, use them, just plant a bit more lavishly.

More Odds & Ends

Let us then be up and doing
With a heart for any fate,
Still achieving, still pursuing,
Learn to Labor, and to wait.
— Henry Wadsworth Longfellow

Labor Day always seems to be a true turning point in the year: the end of summer, the beginning of a completely new season with its attendant cares and concerns for the gardener, even perhaps time for a little rest, with accent on the little. There is so much to do, and so many things to worry about. What will go wrong next? But if you prepare ahead for all the emergencies of life, you do so at the expense of present joy. However, I'll give you a few suggestions from my own list of "Things To Do."

The asparagus bed should be weeded and mulched, and any brown growth cut to the ground, but not the green, as it is still feeding the roots. I like to give it a light fertilizing now with 5-10-10, and again in the spring. Raspberries can be pruned now, cutting the old bearing stalks to the ground, removing suckers and weeds too. Wait until the spring to fertilize, as the plants are quieting down for their winter rest.

My tomato crop this year is plentiful, almost too much so, as I seem to have bowls and trays for tomatoes everywhere, in various stages of ripening. They should not be completely ripened on the vine, as they lose sugar and flavor in the process. They should be picked as they are turning from orange to red, and kept at sixty to seventy degrees in normal light, not on a sunny window sill, and, of course, never in the refrigerator. There have been some problems this year with the tops, which do not ripen and are best just sliced off. I think the cloudy, foggy weather we had in July may be the cause, but like so many other garden mysteries, who knows the answer? One can only guess.

If you have more green peppers than you can eat, remember that they are very easy to freeze. Just chop or slice, freeze on a cookie sheet until solid, and pack into plastic bags. Apparently, however, we Americans don't know how to eat them. John Gale, the owner of Stokes Seeds, scolds," If Americans would just leave their green peppers on the vine and eat them when they are ripe! Eating green peppers is like eating green apples; they don't taste good and they give you gas." So let your peppers ripen on the vine till they begin to change color, and like tomatoes, keep them out of the refrigerator, which ruins the flavor and turns them to "plastic."

Compost

Compost, which seems to be a magic word nowadays, is not a commercial fertilizer, but because it is decaying vegetable matter it supplies nearly every chemical needed by plants. It improves soil texture, holds moisture, and, being dark colored, even absorbs heat. But I like to think of it as paying back to the garden all the bounty we take from it.

Garden catalogues are full of fancy gadgets for making compost, and being a gullible soul when the garden is concerned, I have several. But I still remember the compost I made for many years out on Breezy Point, where the garden had to be surrounded with snow fence against the southwest summer gales. Behind the garage I drove four stakes into the ground in a three-by-three foot square, put some old wire fencing around them, and just dumped all my weeds and kitchen vegetable waste there, plus an occasional shovelful of soil and a good handful of lime, and later the old bean plants, bolted lettuce, whatever was left after the garden cleanup. Next spring I sifted out wheelbarrow loads of perfect compost, and what hadn't decomposed was the start for the next batch. I like wire especially, as it is easy to stick a spading fork in through the sides of the pile and give it a lift for aeration.

A great natural fertilizer: pack weeds and leaves of trees into a large tub and add water (rainwater is best, if available). Soak for ten to fourteen days. Minerals leach out and make a wonderful liquid fertilizer.

Weeding my big vegetable garden is not over yet, but everything is looking better. There is a mountain of mixed weeds and soil on a tarp, wilted down and ready for the compost pile. I have several of these disposable areas, including a fancy Kemp revolving barrel on a stand, and find all of them productive, although some of them take longer than others. After all, we have to dump these dug weeds somewhere.

Next spring's compost will be a mixture of weeds we are struggling with, plus vegetable and fruit scraps from the kitchen, even paper egg cartons. Rule of thumb: If it comes from a plant, compost it. If it comes from an animal, throw it out, except for cow, horse, or chicken manure and eggshells.

Strange things happen if compost is left to its own devices. There is an odd-looking snapdragon blooming on one pile, with open up-facing blossoms (a new sport?), and the bin at the end of my garden path has two tomato plants growing out of the side slits, variety yet to be discovered. It is comforting to know that a little sloppiness in the garden can pay off in exciting ways.

For me, one of the hazards of summer driving on Block Island is not so much the bikes and mopeds, as the endless urge to snoop at other people's gardens as I go along the road, not to mention the compulsion to trespass a bit for a closer look. Gardeners are friendly souls and do not seem to take offense at this, in fact they are usually happy to show off a bit and to discuss problems and share ideas. I have made new friends and learned a lot from them. Occasionally I get some strange and thought-provoking questions to answer, i.e., "Which is better, compost or manure?" Thinking this over, I have come to the conclusion that the ingredients are the same, but the processing is different, and perhaps the "end" results are of equal value.

Of course weeding is always with us, but if you have been thorough up till now, the worst should be over, except for purslane, which loves hot, dry weather, but is so ornamental, edible too, that I hate to hoe it out. Gardeners have a lot of dependent living things all crying for attention, and it is impossible to take care of everything. But we must not feel guilty to let some of them struggle on their own. As we try for perfection, being tired at times is inevitable. Exhaustion is a choice!

Perennials

Early fall is the best time to make over the perennial beds for several reasons, the first being that the weather is cooler and bugs that bite are at a minimum. The soil is warm and should be in excellent condition after a summer's cultivation. The most important part of a healthy growing plant is the root system, and fall planting really gives the root system a break. In the early spring when the gardening frenzy hits most of us, the ground is apt to be cold and wet, and in the late spring the hot sun and longer days encourage top growth at the expense of the roots, but in the fall the reverse is true. And don't forget that even after we have a frost, plant roots continue to develop until the ground really freezes, down where they are, which often never happens on Block Island. So when spring finally arrives, your perennials are all ready to get to work producing flowers.

Soil

The soil under your plants is like the foundation of your house, and on it depends the health and beauty of your garden. A neat, tidy surface with poor soil underneath may impress people, but it won't fool your plants. Perennials, especially, need a deeply prepared soil to a depth of eighteen inches, and it must not only contain the necessary nutrients for plant growth, but should be loose and porous so that the roots can go down after food and moisture. Soil that is too heavy or too sandy should be improved by adding humus in the form of well-rotted manure, compost, or the ever-handy peat moss. It is a waste of time and money to add commercial fertilizer in the fall, except to give late-blooming plants a quick fix, as it will be mostly leached away by spring. Bonemeal is the ideal fall fertilizer for flower gardens. It is very slowacting, absolutely harmless in any amount, and has a lightly sweetening effect. Agway still carries it.

How do we know whether or not we need lime? I have two probes (available from most garden centers). When inserted three-and-a-half inches into the soil, one will register the pH (lime content), the other the fertility. The fertility probe reads "too low, ideal, too high," but does not pinpoint what is missing. But I know my soil and find these very helpful. There are more complicated soil-testing-kits too, expensive, not easy to interpret, and not very accurate. Also, the chemicals they use must be carefully stored and frequently replaced. The best bet if you really feel that your soil is ailing is a soil test done by the experts. The University of Rhode Island (URI) in partnership with the University of Massachusetts at Amherst (UMASS) will test your pH, and levels of nitrogen, phosphorous, and potassium, and will advise you how to correct any deficiencies. The cost is $8 for each test. To take a sample, dig six trowels-full from various locations and put the soil on a newspaper to dry. Enclose a note with your sample, telling what you intend to grow in the area to be tested, i.e lawns, flowers, vegetables. There is a phone number for information on how and where to send your soil sample in the "Garden Resources" section of this book.

Dividing—When?

How often should perennials be divided? This is a matter that seems to puzzle many people, and I have found that it doesn't help much to respond, "When they need it."

There are two major reasons for dividing perennials: one, to increase a choice variety that is scarce or expensive to buy, and two, to increase the health of a plant that has grown too large for its location, with a resulting reduction in bloom. Peonies fall into the first group, iris into the second. In general, any plant that has made a big, round clump with a hard, woody center, or where the blooms are small and scarce, needs dividing. This also increases hardiness, and improves resistance to insects and disease. Iris is a perfect example, as the clump always dies in the center, and new shoots grow on the outside. If left alone, borers will find their way to the old center and gradually kill the plant. Do not ever add these old discards to your compost pile, as they carry eggs of borers, and fungus spores. They should be burned, if possible.

How

The easiest type of plant to divide is one that develops many crowns, each with its own roots. This group includes phlox, primroses, coral bells, Shasta daisies, and many others. To separate these, dig the clump with a spading fork and shake the soil off the roots. Discard the hard center and use only the new growth around the perimeter. Then with scissors or sharp knife, cut back the tops to about three inches and the roots to four inches. Remove any hard, woody roots, and discard any plants showing signs of disease or rot. Replant the divisions about eighteen inches apart, being careful to set the crowns at the proper level. Do not make your divisions too small if you want lots of bloom the following season. About four or five crowns for each plant is a good size. This is the perfect time to feed them, with a handful of slow-acting bonemeal worked into the soil beneath.

There are some perennials that resist our most careful attempts at division, but will thrive on rough treatment. The astilbes, or spireas, belong to this group. Even a sharp knife is baffled by their hard, woody roots, but a spade driven through the center of the clump, preferably by a size twelve foot, will usually prevail. The divisions won't look like much, but never fear, this plant is one of the hardiest in the garden.

Peonies should be handled more carefully. This perennial can grow for many years without disturbance, but if you wish to increase a fine variety divide it now. Shake off the soil and cut the clump carefully apart, leaving at least three eyes to each division (the eyes look like sprouts on potatoes). Prune the long roots to a length practical for planting, about eight inches, and reset with the highest eye not more than two inches under the surface. Better dig in a generous serving of bonemeal and compost under the reset, and, of course, they need full sun to do their best. It is a wise precaution to dust all cut surfaces with sulphur to prevent rot.

Platycodons may be divided in the same manner as peonies, but my experience indicates that they are best tackled in the spring, as they are subject to rot when disturbed in the fall. Bleeding hearts may be handled like peonies. Don't let the pulpy shredded-looking roots alarm you, as it is characteristic of this plant. Contrary to all appearances, there is plenty of life in them.

Most perennials should be planted in groups of three, or five if you have enough room, and give them space, eighteen inches apart, as they will increase in size with time. Accent plants, like peonies, poppies, and lilies, may be planted singly.

If you are happy with your present garden arrangement, replant all divisions promptly, water well, and remember to keep spring blooming bulbs back in the border. But perhaps you would like to reorganize your flower beds. If so, heel in your divided plants in trenches in the vegetable garden, and water well. They will be safe there while you decide how to move your "garden furniture" around.

New Friends

The fall catalogues are arriving with their usual tempting pictures of bulbs and perennials. This is a fine time to check over your gardens with an eye to more summer bloom next year. Order early and plant promptly when they arrive, giving them some compost, bonemeal, or well-rotted manure if you have it. Dehydrated manure is always available and seems to work equally well.

Why not try a few new ones? There are many with very long blooming periods: a day lily called Stella D'Oro, which is a lovely golden yellow and low growing; the achilleas, available in pink, lavender, and gold, very hardy and also valuable for dried arrangements, the sedum Autumn Joy, planted last fall in my border and a blaze of color now; and a fairly new veronica of medium height called Sunny Border Blue. This last is of particular interest to me as it was hybridized by a man I worked for, at his nursery during World War II.

Several years ago I planted a bed of Asiatic lilies for cutting, mixed varieties from Park Seed, and have found them to be an exciting adventure. They have a long blooming period, starting in early July, some even just now in bud. They are completely hardy, and of course the most appealing can be moved to the flower border in early fall for next summer's bloom. This is what I love about perennials. There is always something coming into bloom and other plants going to rest, leaving foliage that enhances the overall picture, an ongoing procession of beauty, starting with spring bulbs and ending with chrysanthemums and hardy asters, and, yes, a few annuals to fill in.

Groundsel

Block Island seems to be especially blessed with masses of white flowers, shad, beach plum, *Rosa rugosa* in the spring, and now in the fall, the groundsel coming into bloom. I first became aware of this shrub on the Eastern Shore of Maryland where we always spent a few days with our daughter on the way down to

Florida in October. They call it *waterbush* there, and with good reason, as it grows all around wetlands, especially salt marshes. You will see it here at its best on the shores of the Salt Pond, opposite the Scotch Beach area, and near Sachem Pond, but it tucks itself into every nook where it can be sure of cool, wet feet. It is a member of the aster family, and is found along the coastal areas from Massachusetts to Florida, and west to Texas and Mexico. It is a lovely, delicate harbinger of fall days to come.

Does the "wind-down" of the gardening season really mean much less work? Do we really want it to? My feelings of self-esteem always seem to be higher after a productive hour or two in the garden, which leads me to believe that basically people do not enjoy wasting time. This is possibly a New England conclusion, as on my refrigerator door I have an old Spanish proverb that reads:"How beautiful it is to do nothing, and then to rest afterward."

October

O suns and skies and clouds of June,
And flowers of June together,
Ye cannot rival for one hour
October's bright blue weather.
      — Helen Hunt Jackson

Lovely October weather, the best time of the year on Block Island for those of us who love peace, sunny days, blue ocean, and more time to enjoy the outdoors without the pressures of time flying by too fast! Our lawns are green again, and the garden soil moist and dark, inviting chores put off earlier because of the drought, and what a relief not to be dragging hoses and soil soakers around! But the fall days are slipping by, and there is still lots to be done in the garden. Here are a few suggestions to fill up those odd moments when your conscience won't let you sit in the sun doing nothing.

Roses should be ordered now for November planting, and the soil prepared to receive them. Dig deep, and enrich the lower level with well-rotted manure, or bonemeal mixed with compost. If you have a peony bed, you can set lily bulbs between the peonies for bloom later in the summer, so order the bulbs now for planting at the end of this month.

Dahlias may be dug and stored now. Dig them carefully so as not to break their poor necks; do not pull them up by the stalks. It is a good idea to set them upside down for a day or two, so that the moisture in the hollow stems can drain out, instead of into the tubers where it can cause rot. They should be stored in a cool, dry place, packed in damp sand or peat moss.

I have had many questions on the treatment and storage of tuberous-rooted begonias. They should be taken up and washed free of soil, with the stems left on temporarily. Set the plants in a cool, dry place, and after about ten days the stem will disjoint itself naturally. Never cut it, or break it off by force. If a tuber is cut in digging, expose it to sun and air and it will heal itself. When tubers are perfectly clean and dry, after about two weeks, they may be stored in flats, or in a coffee can if you have only one or two. Place them in layers with dry sand or peat moss between, and store uncovered in a temperature of about fifty degrees.

Some of us already have residents in the garage awaiting our attention, the dormant amaryllis bulbs from last season, which should be potted up now for bloom this winter. These really need larger pots only every other year, as overpotting will discourage bloom. However, if they are in plastic pots, I'd give them a better home. Mine always get so top-heavy that tipping over is a constant danger. If you repot them into a clay pot with an inch of pebbles in the bottom, they and you will be happier. The pot should be only about an inch larger in diameter than the bulb, and the upper half of the bulb left exposed. Water and wait patiently, and don't worry if the leaves come first, as the flower will follow. If you turn the pot frequently, you will avoid the "leaning tower" problem.

Houseplants

If the calendar doesn't tell us so, the chilly days and cold nights of the past week bring the message that summer is really over, and if our houseplants haven't been brought inside by now, they should be tended to at once. This is the time to take inventory in a hard-hearted and unsentimental manner. There are gardeners so kind that they cannot bear to part with a single plant they have tended, or neglected as the case may be, whether a variety with no claim to beauty (a poor thing, but mine own) or so feeble that it is barely alive (where there's life, there's hope). If you must keep these specimens, relegate them to an isolation ward. You should really keep only those plants that you would be anxious to buy if you were starting from scratch.

Plants need repotting if roots are protruding out of the bottom, or if the pot sounds hollow when tapped, a sign of the plant being rootbound. After a thorough watering, tap the plant out of its pot, and take a good look. Don't be afraid to prune the roots and tops too, so that the plant may be reset in the same size container.

I find that most commercial potting soils are too finely processed, and the addition of some peat moss, perlite, and a little dehydrated cow manure will improve their ability to encourage strong root growth, which, as we all know, is the basis for a healthy plant. Do not fertilize at this time, as the plant must be allowed to adjust slowly to its new growing conditions.

Check plants for insects, especially aphids and white fly. You can slosh them in soapy water and spray insecticide with a freedom outdoors that would cause havoc indoors. In fact, a regular weekly bath in a mild soapy solution will keep foliage plants looking extra clean and healthy. A roasting pan makes a fine bathtub. Soil is held in place by holding a wad of foil or newspaper over the surface of the pot with one hand, and swishing the plant on its side in the solution. Do not subject fuzzy plants like African violets to this treatment, as they are catlike in objecting to water on their fur.

The most potent single factor in making plants miserable indoors is the dryness of the air. Therefore if they are brought into the house before it is necessary to use artificial heat for our own comfort, they have a little time to adapt to their changed climate. There are easy ways to provide humidity all winter for your plants, and the benefits for doing so are more than worth the bother. Keep a small spray bottle handy and mist them daily. A tray filled with pebbles and water is a fine base for groups of plants. It is important, however, that the pots do not sit in the water which will gradually rot the root systems. I use a marvelous waffle-like plastic sheet called egg crate. It is clean, light weight, and may be kept free of mildew by an occasional addition of a little Clorox to the water. This product can be cut to any size with a sharp saw, and is available at building-supply sources. Trays to hold it are found wherever light stands are sold.

I have always had the happiest results using the common, unglazed clay pots. But try to find them! Most of mine are very old and have harbored a wide variety of indoor plants. They allow the soil to breathe, and to drain properly, which minimizes the dangers of overwatering. And they are easily cleaned by a good soaking in a pail of water with a little Clorox added, after which the buildup of salts inside the rim may be quickly scraped off with a putty knife.

I suspect that overwatering is the most common cause of houseplant mortality. When the soil looks dry on top, it doesn't necessarily mean that the root area needs water. In truth, to grow good, healthy houseplants one must be willing to be a nurse. I have an eight-inch probe (instamatic moisture meter), which may be inserted into the soil to register on a dial the moisture condition deep down in the pot. It comes with a useful pamphlet showing the optimum reading on the scale for all types of plants. Most garden centers and some hardware stores carry this handy gadget. Mine is at least ten years old and still works to perfection.

For some real fun and excitement during the long, dark winter, a light stand is high on the list. It is amazing how much color and beauty a four-foot table model can create, and of course it is perfect for starting seeds in the early spring when the houseplants may be moved to a sunny window.

If you are longing for a few new smiling faces to appear among your old friends, treat yourself to some new plants. There is a marvelous houseplant company not too far from us: Logee's Greenhouses in Danielson, CT, about twenty miles north of New London on Route I-395. They have a fascinating catalogue, and ship plants expertly packed in perfect condition. The catalogue is $3, a pleasure to read. See the "Garden Resources" section in the back of the book for their contact information.

I find the old standbys my favorites: geraniums, begonias, ivy, philodendrons and marantas, but also have good luck with cyclamens and cape primroses. This fall I am treating myself to a clivia, a beautiful and undemanding plant with sensational blooms. I had two very old clivias, much-loved denizens of my shady patio in Florida. They would have joined my old hoya "up north" if they had not succumbed to overwatering one summer by a kind caretaking neighbor. That is about the only treatment they will not tolerate. Clivia is a relative of amaryllis, but does not go dormant. The dark green, strap-like leaves are crisp and ornamental, and the bloom, usually in the spring, is gorgeous, large umbels of fragrant salmon pink, orange, or yellow flower clusters on sturdy stalks. They are rather expensive to buy but will delight you for many years to come with a minimum of care. Clivias, natives of Africa, are named for the empire-building Clivden family.

> Listen: The wind is rising,
> And the air is wild with leaves,
> We have had our summer evenings,
> Now for October eves!
>   — Humbert Wolfe

Seasons at Sea Meadow

Patience

The garden season seems to be drawing to a close for this year and what a challenge it has been for us all. Last winter's storms left us with wind damage to shrubs and trees, and terrible beach erosion. Spring was very late, and very wet too, delaying early planting for many of us whose gardens, like mine, are in low-lying locations and were flooded. Then, when we finally began to enjoy the first flowers and veggies, we were hit by the worst summer drought I can remember. According to my daily garden journal, from mid-June to mid-September we had about one-and-a-half inches of rain, and the whole summer was very hot and breezy with low humidity, fine for vacationers, but a nightmare for gardeners. Finally about mid-September the fall rains came, including the usual equinoctial nor'easter, and then the first frost on October 24. We are now enjoying the finest Indian summer weather I can remember. The point of all this is that our spring bloom was gorgeous—apple trees, lilacs, shad—and the blackberries huge and sweet. I had delphiniums and hollyhocks six feet tall, and still have snapdragons and alyssum blooming in my borders. Vegetables, too, were plentiful and delicious. Altogether, I have never seen the gardens better, or more beautiful. Perhaps there is a message here for us. As Emerson said, "Adopt the pace of nature; her secret is patience."

October Chores

These last warm days are perfect for finishing up outside chores, cleaning out the shed and garage, raking leaves, filling the birdfeeders, and other pleasant activities. Here are a few reminders. All dead annuals, tomato vines, et cetera, should be pulled up and composted. Cut off the bean plants when they stop bearing, but let the roots stay to supply nitrogen to the soil. Leave carrots in the ground with a heavy mulch of hay, for an early spring treat. Beets, too, may be kept this way well into early winter.

Weeds may be loosened up with a scuffle hoe or spading fork and raked out, but if they are seedy do not put them in the compost, as it is almost impossible now to get the pile hot enough to kill the seeds, which will come back to haunt you next spring.

Perennials should be cut back to about three inches. Those little stalks will hold hay or mulch against the wind, but do not put it on until the ground freezes hard. If put on too early, all the field mice in the countryside will make your garden their winter home, but if you wait till the ground is really frozen, they have usually taken up residence elsewhere. The real purpose of a winter mulch on the garden is not to keep it warm, but to keep it cold, just as vegetables are put in the Deepfreeze to preserve them. When plants alternately freeze and thaw through the winter, they tend to heave up out of the ground, and either the roots are broken off or the plant is raised so high that the sun and winds of February and March dry out the root system. The mulch keeps the sun from striking the surface of the soil and thawing it. On the the other hand, carrots and beets may be harvested all winter if protected by six inches of mulch, put on *before* the ground freezes.

Here on Block Island we have some winters when the soil never really freezes more than an inch or two, and we must do the best we can in making these momentous decisions.

If you are an orderly person, you will enjoy cleaning up the vegetable garden, and composting the debris. If you pile it all up to dry out a bit and then put it through a shredder, it will be easier to handle. I have a Junior Tomahawk Troy Built, which can be wheeled around and is fairly easy to start, although I do wish my arms were four inches longer for that initial pull of the cord.

The flower beds also should have attention. Yesterday I pulled up a wheelbarrow load of petunias, with apologies to the small flowers still bravely blooming at the tips of those long, straggly branches. Perennials should be cut back to encourage fall growth by letting air and light into their crowns, and then a thorough weeding and later mulching of the whole area will pay dividends later. Many of the weeds in the flower beds are perennials, and if left will make for a miserable spring job. All this may beem like a lot of work, but it may be done at one's leisure, and you won't feel like it when the weather gets colder, or especially next spring when you are not in as good physical shape as now. As Mark Twain points out, "Everyone wants to go to heaven [no weeds] but no one wants to follow the route to get there."

Bulbs

One of the most worrisome aspects of gardening, for me at least, is the presence of a box of plant material, at this time of year usually bulbs, ordered months ago in a moment of optimism and now taking up space in the garage awaiting my ministrations. But these lovely, crisp, bright days tempt us to stay outdoors as much as possible. Bulb planting is really not hard work, and the thought of our gardens looking next spring like those in the magazines fills us with a sort of euphoria peculiar to gardeners. All bulbs should be planted by now, except for tulips, which can go in as long as your hands will take the cold. There is no need to fertilize them, as the blooms are already inside the bulbs. So wait till next spring to feed them, when the foliage is showing.

Several days ago I planted one hundred crocus bulbs in about an hour, in the lawn up along my stone wall by the following method: I slid a spading fork about two inches deep on a slant, lifting the sod in uneven patches, stirred up the exposed soil with a good hand-ful of bonemeal, set the little bulbs firmly about three inches apart in groups of various colors, replaced the sod, and walked on it. Tomorrow, groups of scillas, pink, blue, and white, go into the back of my flower border where the planting will be easy, and some special daffodils in a yet-undetermined, very special spot. I can hardly wait for spring!

If you are naturalizing daffodils, remember that nature doesn't plant in rows! The most effective way to plant them, and other small bulbs too, is to toss them outward from a basket or pail, and plant them where they land.

Tools

Tools are our friends and should be treated with proper care, which they will repay many times over. Mine are all over fifty years old. They have solid ash handles, steel tines and blades, and a lovely patina from years of use. They are always put away clean, and hung up in their proper place. I have a weeding fork, like a hand-size spading fork, which traveled to New Zealand and back with me in the seventies. It caused a sensation at the security check in Honolulu until I explained that it was not a weapon. Rust is the worst enemy of tools, but very easy to prevent by rinsing and then drying the tines with an old towel lightly coated with mineral oil or a little kerosene. If you put your tools away cleaned and oiled in the fall, the spring will be made brighter by their shining greet-ings, ready for work!

Take an hour or so on one of these gray, fall days to make some notes in your journal about your successes and failures, what needs changing next year in the flower garden from the standpoint of color, height, and season of bloom, which vegetables should be relocated to prevent soil problems, planting dates, et cetera. The list of odds and ends to be checked is endless, but don't panic: we still have all of October to enjoy, puttering about in a leisurely manner.

Last Sunday in church at the end of the service, a friendly man in the pew behind me tapped me on the shoulder and said, "May I please see your thumbs?" Of course I laughed and obliged, and was reminded that the myth of the occult green thumb still lives, but the truth is that all anyone needs for success with plants and gardens is a true interest and an observing eye.

Feathered Friends

This has been a wonderful year for birds, and just now they seem to be exploding from every thicket as they head for warmer climes, after a few days of R and R here on the Island. It is sad to relate that there are always a few casualties when the migrants fly into the big glass doors or bay windows here. Last year these claimed a cedar waxwing, two golden-crowned kinglets, a myrtle warbler, a black-throated blue warbler (so beautiful), and a red-eyed vireo, all now laid to rest in my garden. But last spring I found a solution to this mayhem in a catalogue from Lee Valley Tools: transparent decals of spiderwebs, eight inches square, and easy to apply. These are barely noticeable from indoors but I have had no casualties so far, and the migrations are nearly over. Hallelujah!

If you are an early riser, you have a chance to witness a rare phenomenon that once seen is never forgotten. I refer to the "Green Flash." I first experienced this in Florida at sunset. There, if the sky is crystal clear with no clouds or haze on the horizon, there is a green flash of light just as the upper rim of the sun disappears into the sea, the Gulf of Mexico on the west coast where we lived. This flash is instantaneous; if you blink you could miss it! Here on Block Island I see the horizon only in the east, and the miracle is different. There is no flash, but just for a second or two as the sun comes up out of the ocean, it is as green as an emerald. The sun rises about a quarter to seven now, and a northwest wind will usually give a clear horizon. Watch for this lovely sight, and be patient!

Now that daylight saving time is gone and our sunny afternoons are shortened, it is about time to straighten our backs and leave our gardens to sleep and dream of spring. The clear night skies are full of stars, and the season is winding down, but take care! Halloween is nigh!

You better draw the door bolt
And look what you're about!
The goblins will get you
If you don't watch out!

A thousand murky goblins
Are loose upon the air,
Are frisking diabolically
Above the Little Bear,
Are dropping from the Swan's wing
And coasting down the Dragon,
and tipping up the Dipper
As though it were a flagon,
And now they're climbing up the sky
And perching on the Lion,
Or shaking flakes of silver

Seasons at Sea Meadow

From the sword of old Orion,
And leaping onto Pegasus
And swinging from his tail,
And scattering the Pleiades
Like bits of shining hail.

You'd better pull the curtains close
And make the shutters tight:
A thousand murky goblins
Are loose upon the night!
          - JBF

November & December

The melancholy days are come, the saddest of the year,
Of wailing winds and naked woods, and meadows
   brown and sere,
The robin and the wren are flown, gone from the shrubs
   the jay,
And from the treetop calls the crow through all the
   gloomy day.
   — William Cullen Bryant

It seems to me that one of the most charming aspects of our Island is the frequent disguise perpetrated on us by the weather. This October has been the finest in memory: warm, sunny, lovely sunrises and sunsets, and so many birds, even four bluebirds reported! Rainfall has been sparse, but with the short days and cool nights, the soil is still moist and easy to weed, also perfect for planting bulbs, shrubs, and resetting divided perennials. The lilacs have new buds; little volunteer seedlings are sprouting in the flower garden. We could be in the middle of May! It has been a period of pleasant outdoor work, but by four in the afternoon the sun leaves us, and it is time to pick up the garden tools and settle inside for the long evening. This morning as I write this it is gusting up to 60 mph on my wind gauge, and I'm sure we will have no boats or mail. There is still much to be done outdoors, but perhaps November will be kind and grant us a few more mild days. Gentleness in weather is the best, as in people too.

Seasons at Sea Meadow

When the wind is howling around the eaves and rain pelting the windows, we can still garden by making notes about this year's successes and failures, and by planning for next year. I keep a map of my garden beds each year, so I know what grew when and where, and can make the necessary plans for next spring's crop rotation. The disasters and bright spots of past years provide interesting reading on a dark, wintry day. We can almost hear the catbirds talking to us, and smell the warm rich earth and the fragrant spring breezes.

Last August 15 I set out some gladiolus bulbs, still kicking around unplanted in the garage. Of course it was late, but not a total failure! They came up promptly, grew fast, and by November 1 had begun to put up tightly budded spikes. Just before the first frost here on November 8, I cut them all and put them in a deep container in the garage. As I write these notes on November 17, I have two big vases full of flowers in my living room, and more to come in the cool garage. A pleasant, gorgeous surprise!

It is amazing how many things can go wrong in our gardens or not live up to our expectations, as we continue to seek that nebulous nirvana of perfection, but that is the endless fascination and addictive intrigue of gardening. One good thing about being old is that you won't have to live with your mistakes forever!

The misty earth below is wan and drear,
The baying winds chase all the leaves away
As cruel hounds pursue the trembling deer;
It is a solemn time, the sunset of the year.
     — R.H. Stoddard

The "baying winds" have removed all the leaves from my two large maple trees to parts unknown, a loss to my compost pile, but I have yet to see a deer trembling at the evening chase of my two little wire-haired dachshunds. They just remove themselves temporarily from the nuisance into the Maze and come out later to browse. Fine exercise and lots of fun for the dogs, however! Barkis, my seven-year-old male, is always on the alert for trouble. Living alone as I do, I find it extremely comforting to have a "man of the house" about, to protect me, the little female canine, and the premises in general, including the car, from all invasions of illegal humans and varmints. In fact, dogs are important members of the community on Block Island where, out-of-season, the preferred mode of transportation is the pickup truck, usually with a friendly Lab in the back protecting the toolbox.

> From gold to gray,
> Our mild, sweet day
> Of Indian Summer fades too soon;
> But tenderly
> Above the sea
> Hangs, white and calm, the hunter's moon.
> — John Greenleaf Whittier

Varmints

The deer-hunting season starts soon, and I have reluctantly opened my meadow to it. This is the first year I've had real trouble with deer, as my vegetable garden is securely fenced, and until now Barkis has kept them away from the house area, but no longer. Basically I love all animals, and recognize the fact that Homo sapiens is one of them, but enough is enough! It takes me back to forty years ago in Wilton, CT when we saw red foxes, woodchucks, squirrels, and rabbits in our meadow, but no deer. The worst pests were chipmunks, those little rats made cute by Disney.

They ate my perennials underground, dined on my carrots and beets, lunched on bulbs, and worst of all kept up a constant "cheep cheep cheep" from all the surrounding stone walls. One day, I took a little 22-caliber shotgun, sat on the terrace, and eliminated about of them, and never saw another near my gardens. I am fond of snakes, too, but that same year in spring I shot a six-foot black snake who was up in a high hemlock hedge eating baby robins out of their nest, and, perhaps wrongly, have never felt guilty about either incident. It occurred to me the other day that we can be thankful that the deer keep silence about our problems with them. Imagine what a bedlam Block Island would be if they roared like lions or howled like wolves!

Winter Residents

This past October gave us the loveliest weather I can ever remember or imagine on Block Island, one sunny mild day after another, but then November blew in, bringing two nor'easters, cold nights, and raw, windy days, dark by 4:30 in the afternoon and inky black at 5:30 in the morning, my usual rising time.

My bird feeders, banished to the garage during the recent, terrible winds, are now back outside my big bay window, and I am treated to endless entertainment, thereby. This year, to my surprise, I have several red-breasted nuthatches, after bluebirds, perhaps, my favorites. When I lived on Breezy Point I always had a pair nesting in the pines by the vegetable garden, and their plaintive little "yank yank" was a familiar sound all summer. They are smaller than the white-breasted, with a black stripe through the eye and a white stripe above, the breast a lovely, pale orangey pink. They eat insects from the bark of trees, but also like black-oil sunflower seed. Birds seem to enjoy dining together: cardinals, finches, white-throated sparrows, even the big mourning doves.

Only those loudmouthed brats, the blue jays, scatter them. But the little nuthatch lights on the feeder, selects a sunflower seed, and zooms off to eat it leisurely, by first embedding it in the bark of a nearby tree. According to the Cornell University Lab of Ornithology it is estimated that eighty-six million people provide food for birds. Yet there is no real evidence that feeders are beneficial to wild bird populations. So why do so many people spend so much money to feed birds? Because it's fun!

A Bit of Force

Many of the Christmas catalogues deluging us now offer blooming plants, pots of flowering bulbs, and other out-of-season high-priced delights. It is easy to force bulbs, and fun too. The key word here is *temperature*. If you do not have a cold frame, a trench in the garden will suffice. The bulbs should be kept cold but not frozen. Shallow pots called *bulb pans* are best, but not essential. Place your bulbs close together, but not touching, and cover with soil. Then place them in your frame or trench and cover with a good, thick layer of leaves, straw, or mulch. Leave them there for six to seven weeks to form roots, then bring them inside to a cool dark place (fifty to fifty-five degrees), perhaps an unheated garage with a carton or basket over them. When leaves emerge, gradually add light, and water sparingly. They can come inside to be enjoyed when the blooms emerge. Tulips and daffodils are easy, crocuses are always cheery, and hyacinths will perfume a whole room.

Holiday Greens

A check this morning of the thermometer outside my kitchen window (twenty-eight degrees) restores my faith in the veracity of the woolly bears as weather prophets. It is cold, and our Indian summer, which comes after the first frost, is a dream, but the approaching holiday season with so much to do makes a respite from outdoor work very welcome.

Here on Block Island many of us make our own Christmas decorations, and we are fortunate in having a wealth of fine native material to use. Back in the fifties, when I had my little nursery business in Wilton, CT, we had a ton of balsam fir shipped down by truck in November from Vermont, and indeed it is a wonderful soft evergreen to handle, with needles that stay green and fresh and never drop. Here, spruce, black and white pine, juniper, hemlock, and many other greens are at hand, and even perhaps some balsam fir, although it prefers a colder climate. The materials for decorating are everywhere: cones, bittersweet, bayberry, black alder berries, even dried flowers from our summer gardens. Wreaths can be made ahead of time and hung in a cool, damp spot like a garden shed, to be embellished later when a creative mood hits us.

There are many techniques and materials for wreathmaking, even coathangers are possible, but most commercial wreaths are made on metal rings of various sizes, the greens fastened to them with spool wire, and the decorations either tied on with florist wires, or wired to wooden picks and poked into the base wires. You can get wreathmaking supplies sent over to the Island from Agway or Smith's Flower Shop (see "Garden Resources" in the back of the book for their contact information), or check in with our local Goose and Garden shop.

Before starting your wreath, cut the greens into pieces six or seven inches long. Fasten the end of your spool wire to the ring, and lay your greens on the curve and to each side, fastening every three or four pieces by winding the spool wire securely under and over the ring, two or three times. It is wise to have the first few pieces a little longer, as the finishing pieces must be tucked under them. If the wreath is to be hung on a glass door, it should be turned over as you go, and a few pieces of greens worked on the back to cover the ring. This also makes for a thicker and fluffier wreath. Vary your greens as you work around the ring for a subtle color effect. You can even work in some Colorado blue spruce. I advise wearing heavy gloves when handling this, as the needles are very sharp, but the lovely, blue color is worth it! If your wreath ends up with a few thin spots, just stick in a few greens tied to a pick, or put your bow there. Roping is made by cutting spool wire to the needed length, fastening one end securely, and then tying your greens to it with the spool wire, but it must be made double sided to hang well. If they are wired, cones may be tied in right along with the greens.

When decorating your wreaths it is more effective to use several groups of cones or berries, rather than to "polka-dot" them. White pinecones will open up if put in a warm place, and if you cut them in half with sharp scissors or small clippers, presto! you have flowers. These may be left natural, but they are very pretty if given a little spray paint: white, pale blue, pale yellow, and even sprinkled with glitter while the paint is wet. Wire three or five together with florist's wire and tuck them into your wreath.

Centerpieces are easy to make and lots of fun. All you need is a flat tray or heavy foil, a block of oasis, and some imagination. Greens should be stuck into the oasis starting at the base, and building up, shortening the pieces as you go. Leave a little space on top to imbed three red candles in the center, and decorate with whatever you wish: small Christmas ornaments, foil-wrapped candies, little toys, or just cones and berries. If the oasis is kept moist, this will last throughout the holidays.

As the year and this century draw to a close, let us remember our forebears, Adam and Eve in the Garden of Eden, where perhaps all our love of nature began, or so it seems the Lord intended. Now winter is upon us, a time of early dark and blustery

winds. But before long we will be pouring over the new catalogues, and as the Bible tells us, "The flowers appear on the earth,
and the singing of birds is come."

> The gardening year is winding down
> And autumn leaves are falling fast;
> The time has come to leave the soil,
> To make an end to hours of toil,
> And leave our gardens to the past.
> It's now too late for second guessings
> So let's relax and count our blessings!
>
> Our gratitude for morning light,
> For sunrise beauty in the east,
> The fires of sunset in the west
> With messages of peace and rest,
> The silent beauty of the night,
> The moonpath on the quiet sea,
> Stars like a million scattered birds
> Trailing above their silver flight,
> The lace of spiderwebs at dawn
> And birds' tracks on the dewy lawn,
> For dunes and cliffs, and beach grass too,
> For seagulls drifting over blue,
> For sunny days and cloudy skies,
> For all the birds and butterflies,
> For chickadees who bring us cheer,
> And little dogs who chase the deer.
>
> Kudos and thanks to our higher power
> For every tree and every flower,

For "daffs" in spring and "mums" in fall,
For bushy shrubs and plants that sprawl,
And also those that climb a wall!
For little seedlings here and there,
Thriving in unpolluted air.

Our thanks for welcome rain that falls
And brings an end to days of drought,
Our gratitude for winter snows,
And for the friends who plow us out.

And there are things without a doubt
We're happy to exist without:
Raccoons and woodchucks, nature's thieves,
The farmer's bane, the foes of sheaves,
And squirrels' evil machinations,
Cleaning out our feeding stations;
No skunks, a scarcity of rabbits,
(Tis wiser not to list their habits.)

Oh, who would ever wish to roam
From this lovely Isle we all call home?
With Ogden Nash I must agree!
His final words, to you from me,
"Oh let your future be as lucky as your past,
Oh may every day for a long time not be your last;"

To all my readers, a Merry Christmas, and best wishes for a "bluebird" New Year!

Appendix: Garden Resources

Seeds

Burpee
W. Altee Burpee & Co.
Warminster, PA. 18974
(800) 888-1447

Harris Seeds
60 Saginaw Drive
PO Box 22960
Rochester, NY 14692-2960
(716) 295-3600

Park Seed
1 Parkton Avenue
Greenwood, SC 29647-0001
(800) 845-3369

Shepherd's Garden Seeds
30 Irene Street
Torrington, CT. 06790-6658
(800) 444-6910

Flower Specialists

Cooley's Garden
Tall Bearded Iris
PO Box 126 NT
Silverton, OR   97381
(800) 933-1343

Schreiner's Iris Gardens
3625 Quinaby Rd, NE
Salem, OR 97303-9720
(no phone listing available)

Smith's Flower Shop
136 Beach Street
Westerly, RI 02891
(401) 596-4993

White Flower Farm
PO Box 50
Litchfield, CT. 06759-0050
(800) 503-9624

Appendix: Garden Resources continued

Publications

Avant Gardener
PO Box 489
New York, NY 10028
(no phone listing available)

Bottom Line
c/o Botanical & Herb Reviews
PO Box 1343
Fayetteville, AR 72702
(no phone listing available)

Garden Sampler
7211 Middle Ridge Road
Madison, OH 44057
(no phone listing available)

Soil Testing

University of Rhode Island
Co-op Extension Education Center
(401) 874-1000 / (800) 448-1011
call for instructions & information

Supplies

Agway
90-92 Pershing Avenue
Wakefield, RI 02879
(401) 783-2770

Lee Valley Tools, Ltd
PO Box 1780
Ogdensburg, NY 13669-6780
(800) 871-8158

Logee's Greenhouses
141 North Street
Danielson, CT 06239
(860) 774-8038

Mellinger's Inc.
2310 W. South Range Road
North Lima, OH 44452-9731
(330) 549-9861

Smith & Hawken
PO Box 6900
2 Arbor Lane
Florence, KY 41022-6900
(800) 940-1170

Index

Index continued

Index continued